PLANNING YOUR RETIREMENT

Best wishes!

Bob

PLANNING YOUR RETIREMENT

A Practical Guide for Turning Your Dreams into Reality

ROBERT GERSTEMEIER, CFP®, EA

LIONCREST
PUBLISHING

PLANNING YOUR RETIREMENT

A Practical Guide for Turning Your Dreams into Reality

ISBN   978-1-5445-1315-7 *Paperback*
       978-1-5445-1314-0 *Ebook*

To our three wonderful sons: You make your mom and me so happy and proud of you in all the things that you do. You are the true measure of wealth for both of us. Someday, when there are no more pages to add to our own books of life, know that the three of you will be the best part.

Contents

Disclaimer 9

Acknowledgments 11

Introduction 15

1. The Realities of Retirement 33

2. Start with Where You Are:
   An Analysis of Your Current Situation 51

3. Identify Your Goals 75

4. Insurance: Planning for Catastrophe 87

5. Investing Basics 107

6. The Role of the Government 143

7. Making Your New Paycheck 177

8. Passing On Your Assets 197

9. Turning Theory into Reality 223

   Conclusion 243

   About the Author 251

DISCLAIMER

Information provided in this book is general in nature and does not constitute specific financial advice. Each person's situation is different. Information, the economic environment, and tax laws can, and will, change without notice. Every effort has been made to ensure that the information provided is accurate. Individuals must not rely on this information to make a financial or investment decision. Before making any decision, the author and publisher recommend you consult a financial planner or tax advisor to take into account your particular investment objectives, financial situation, and individual needs. Past performance is not a guarantee of future results.

Certified Financial Planner Board of Standards Inc. (CFP Board) owns the certification marks CFP® and CERTIFIED FINANCIAL PLANNER™ in the United

States, which it authorizes use of by individuals who successfully complete CFP Board's initial and ongoing certification requirements.

ACKNOWLEDGMENTS

I have to start by thanking my wonderful wife, Laura. From reading and editing early drafts to giving me advice on the cover, to keeping the house in order so I could spend time on this book, she was as important to this book getting done as I was. Thank you so much!

Mom and Dad, thank you for raising me with a sense of helping and serving others in life. All the volunteer work you have done in your lives has provided a great example for others to follow. If I ever needed anything, you were always there for me. Thank you!

A special thanks goes out to the people who helped me get into this profession—Ed O'Hara, Frank Nelson, and my other cohorts in those early financial planning classes. Your views, recommendations, and consistent encouragement allowed me to enter this profession in a way that aligned with my beliefs. Thank you!

To Dan Hoffman, my first boss in this profession. I'm not sure I'll ever have a conversation with someone else that touches on prospects for the Cubs that year, instituting a barbell fixed-income strategy, and discussing the finer points of bond convexity. Thank you for your insights, help, and friendship all these years!

I want to thank all the financial planners in the National Association of Personal Financial Advisors (NAPFA) who have helped me over the years. Providing help, guidance, and encouragement to another is one of the greatest gifts of the human spirit. You live that every day in your thoughtful interactions with your clients and fellow professionals.

To the men and women who serve in our nation's military. I know the sacrifices you make every day in your service to our country. Thank you to all those serving and especially your families that love and support you during difficult and often stressful times. My time in the military had a measurable and positive impact on my career and is a direct result of the military professionals I continue to interact with today.

Last, I want to thank all of my clients. I'm honored and

humbled that you have given me the opportunity to serve as your financial advisor. Your trust in my ability to help and guide you has given me a great sense of satisfaction and has allowed me to provide for my family. Thank you, and I look forward to each opportunity to serve you and your families in the future.

Introduction

The New Age of Retirement

When we think of retirement, many of us remember what it was like for our parents or grandparents. They probably worked most of their lives for the same company, and when they reached retirement, that company continued to take care of them in the form of a pension. The company had a board of directors who would decide how much to save and how to invest the pension fund in a way to produce a steady stream of income for the company's retired workers.

That world is mostly a thing of the past. Today, each of us is responsible for our retirement. We not only need to save up for retirement, but we also must figure out how to invest those savings so they will last the rest of our lives.

While many companies will match whatever you save in your 401(k) retirement account (up to a point, of course), the trustees of the retirement plan who used to take care of the investments for you now just decide which investments to put into the company's 401(k) lineup of choices. It's up to you to determine how much to save and where to put that money, both before you retire and after.

Some of the most important decisions of your life are centered on taking care of your retirement. In a sense, you are at sea in a boat all by yourself, and you have to plot your own course. You have to know what direction to sail in and how long it will take to get to your destination. You have to learn how to forecast the weather and gauge the wind. Most importantly, you have to manage all those little disruptions that arise during the trip—the unexpected squalls, the occasional rough seas, and the doldrums, when there is no wind to help you, and it feels like you're going nowhere.

CHALLENGES OF RETIREMENT

Retirement in the United States changed forever when Congress passed the Revenue Act of 1978, which created the first 401(k) plans. Two years later, the IRS gave employees a tax-free way to use salary deductions to fund their 401(k) plans. People loved this. They could transfer money from their gross pay to a retirement account and not have to pay any taxes on the income until years later when they retired and started withdrawing the funds.

Companies also loved 401(k) plans, which were cheaper and more predictable than defined benefit pension plans. Within a few years of the Revenue Act, many large companies switched from offering pension plans to making contributions to their employees' 401(k) plans.

The US Department of Labor watched as that trend accelerated over the next several years. In 1980, for example, nearly a third of all Americans still had a defined benefit pension plan for their retirement and only one in twenty had one of the new 401(k) accounts. By 2010, the Department of Labor found that only about 2 percent of Americans had pensions and more than a third had a 401(k) plan as their primary source of funds for retirement. Nearly 80 percent of all US residents worked for an employer who offered a 401(k) plan. In just thirty years, the retirement landscape had changed dramatically.

The result is that today, if you're fifty-five or so and have been saving for retirement throughout your career, you must decide how to invest those savings so that you have a steady income that covers all your needs after you leave the workforce. Retirement used to be simple: work hard for thirty or forty years, then pick up your gold watch and collect your pension check every month. Now, even in retirement, your work isn't over. You still face difficult questions about how to nurture your nest egg so that it will continue to provide for you over the next thirty years or so.

That's a tall order!

MYTHS ABOUT RETIREMENT

To make matters even more challenging, many prospective retirees leave the workforce believing a number of myths about retirement. Let's take a look at some of those mistaken beliefs.

I'LL ONLY NEED ABOUT 70 PERCENT OF MY PRERETIREMENT INCOME TO LIVE COMFORTABLY AFTER RETIREMENT.

Well, maybe and maybe not. It all depends on your goals and objectives. Do you plan on traveling after retirement? Many people do. What about healthcare and medical expenses? These costs often increase for retirees, and you have to take them into consideration. You may still have a mortgage or a car payment to make. You still have to pay taxes on your income. While it's true that many retirees learn to reduce their spending after retirement, not everyone can.

I WON'T FACE ANY FINANCIAL SURPRISES AFTER RETIREMENT.

What if you need a new roof? What if the car you just paid off breaks down? What if you suffer a major illness? Many people don't take these challenges into consideration or plan ahead for them when thinking about retirement. Despite your detailed planning for the expenses you will face in retirement, unexpected expenses can arise and some of these expenses may be substantial.

NOW THAT I'M RETIRED, I CAN GET CONSERVATIVE WITH MY INVESTMENTS. I'M ONLY GOING TO LIVE TILL I'M SEVENTY, SO I WON'T NEED THAT MUCH MONEY.

The average life expectancy for Americans today is much greater than it was when your parents and grandparents retired. According to the Centers for Disease Control and Prevention, the life expectancy for an American in 1950 was sixty-eight years. Today, it's seventy-nine— and higher in the United Kingdom and Canada (around eighty-two).

If you were going to live for only ten years after you retire, then, yes, you could be as conservative as you want, because you can eat into your principal and it's not going to cause you any problems. Today, thanks to modern medicine and our own healthy habits, many of us will live for another twenty-five or thirty years after we retire. This means we will need an income that can out-pace inflation and cover our financial needs during that time. Accomplishing this requires making wise invest-ment decisions and keeping an eye on those investments.

IT'S EASIER TO START SAVING LATER IN LIFE AFTER I'VE PUT THE KIDS THROUGH COLLEGE AND PAID OFF THE HOUSE. THAT'S WHEN I'LL START FOCUSING ON RETIREMENT.

The problem with this approach is that you miss out on twenty or thirty years of growth in the stock market. Saving and investing early—even if it's just a small amount—will put you way ahead of someone who stops saving at thirty-five and then resumes after the kids are grown. Investing early allows you to reap the benefits of compound interest. Compounding is when you reinvest your earnings, allowing your initial investment to grow exponentially. This is why people like me always encour-age young people to start saving and investing as early as possible!

Time is the Key — Early Savers Win

Investors with modest lifetime incomes can retire in comfort
if a retirement plan is started early. See in the example below
how a late saver can't catch up even after 50 years.

Year	Early Saver	Late Saver
	Deposits $1,000/year at 8%	*Deposits nothing*
1	$1,083	$0
5	$6,397	$0
10	$15,939	$0
	Deposits nothing else, builds at 8%	*Deposits $1,000/year at 8%*
11	$17,267	$1,083
20	$35,471	$15,939
30	$78,934	$51,939
40	$175,656	$130,344
50	$390,895	$306,000

I'VE SAVED $1 MILLION IN MY 401(K) AND I CAN RETIRE
EARLY.

Most people don't think of their 401(k) balance in
spendable after-tax terms. Having $1 million set aside
in a tax-advantaged plan is great, but the reality is that
to spend any of that, you will have to pay taxes on the
money first. That makes a million-dollar portfolio worth
only $750,000 after tax (assuming a 25 percent tax rate).
For many retirees, they overstate the real value of their
(tax-deferred) retirement assets. Having a million in a
401(k) or IRA is not the same as having a million to spend.

MY COMPANY WILL TAKE CARE OF MY HEALTHCARE
NEEDS BEFORE MY SOCIAL SECURITY AND MEDICARE
KICK IN.

Many companies are moving away from offering ongoing healthcare. Even the companies that help early retirees are putting an increasing burden on the shoulders of former workers to cover a portion of that cost. This can represent a significant expense that eats into your savings in the years before you reach full retirement age and begin receiving Medicare benefits at age sixty-five.

RETIREMENT PLANNING IS EASY. I'LL JUST ANALYZE
MY SPENDING FOR ONE YEAR AND THEN SET UP MY
INVESTMENTS TO COVER MY NEEDS. I CAN SET IT AND
FORGET IT.

It's never that easy. The sequence of stock market returns varies significantly and has a major impact on your portfolio's health. You have to pay attention and make adjustments depending on what the market does.

The S&P 500 returns about 10 percent on average, but the returns are often below that over an extended period, such as the first decade of the 2000s. If that decade occurred during the first ten years of your retirement, you would have started eating into your principal much sooner than someone who invested at a different time. To increase the odds you won't run out of money, you would have had to cut back on your spending or do something else to make up for the meager returns. Taking the set-it-and-forget-it approach can produce a disastrous outcome when you least expect it.

I HAVE ENOUGH SAVED TO MAINTAIN MY CURRENT LIFESTYLE IN RETIREMENT.

We will go into this more later, but inflation is the greatest threat to most retirees' standard of living in retirement. For example, assuming just a 3 percent inflation rate, $70,000 annual spending in today's dollars will require nearly $95,000 to buy the same level of goods and services ten years from now. Fifteen or twenty years make this calculation even more dramatic. The point is that most retirees think in only today's dollars and can't fathom what inflation is going to do to their annual spending over time. A major risk would be a burst of inflation (such as in the 1970s) that would materially impact a retiree's real (inflation-adjusted) ability to maintain a lifestyle or level of spending in retirement. I don't want to be all doom and gloom here. It's true that retirement poses challenges that our parents and grandparents perhaps did not face, but that doesn't mean it has to be a frightening or uncertain time. In fact, if you follow some of the steps I will discuss in this book, retirement should be everything you hoped it would be.

KEEPING YOUR SHIP ON COURSE

Although it's true that you, as a future retiree, are responsible for finding the cash flow to fund your weekly or monthly paycheck in retirement, you don't necessarily have to do it alone. This book is designed to help you.

I'll walk you through all the steps I take with my own clients, and you will find that these tasks are not complicated. First, we'll talk about how you can evaluate your current financial situation, then we'll develop reasonable investment goals that fit your needs. Once we zero in on your resources and what your future needs will look like, we'll talk about how you can manage your wealth through a sound, practical investment program.

Along the way, we'll talk about several other issues that confront folks during retirement. Here are a few of the topics we'll explore:

- **How will you fund your paycheck after you stop working?** For most people, retirement income will come from a variety of sources. We'll talk about how to best utilize those, whether they include pensions, Social Security, dividends, or any number of other sources of income available to you after you stop working.
- **How can you minimize your tax obligations?** Remember, you deferred paying taxes for years while

you saved for retirement. Now Uncle Sam wants his cut. We'll discuss strategies for keeping your tax bill as low as possible so you can hold on to those hard-earned savings.

- **How can you protect your assets?** Your nest egg is likely a big source of your future income. We'll talk about the best ways to invest that money so that you can remain confident and secure in retirement regardless of how the stock market behaves.

- **What's the best way to pass on your wealth to your loved ones and heirs?** Retirees who are planning their estate have many options, and we'll talk through those that will work best for your situation.

- **How can I avoid some of the financial mistakes that people make both leading up to and after retirement?** While it's true that retirees sometimes make poor choices—such as getting too conservative with their investments—I'll share investment approaches with you that are straightforward and simple. These will buffer you from unexpected problems.

FINDING A TRUSTED ADVISOR

Many people are concerned about whether or not they have enough wealth to achieve the retirement they envision. Do they have 50 percent of what they need, or do they have 150 percent? This book will not only help you figure that out but will also give you actionable strategies if you fall short. Even if you've saved just 25 percent of what you need in retirement funding, I'll give you some strategies to help make up the difference.

This book will also show you why it's wise to have a trusted advisor to help navigate some of these decisions. You can go it alone, of course, and this book will help you do that. But if you're feeling alone at sea in that boat, you may want to bring on a captain to help guide you. I clearly have a self-interest in recommending this. But I also have your interests in mind; I have a passion for helping my clients achieve their dreams, and I hope this book convinces you that it's wise to have a trusted advisor with you on your journey.

MY OWN JOURNEY

I've worked in financial planning for the last twenty years. Today, I have clients all over the country and offices in Chicago, Cincinnati, and Naples, Florida.

I didn't set out to be a financial planner. As a kid, I dreamed of flying, and in particular, I dreamed of flying off aircraft carriers. I attended Miami University on a naval scholarship and went to flight school in Pensacola.

When the navy retired the type of plane I flew, I transferred to the Pentagon in naval intelligence. While there, I earned my MBA at night. It was around this time that my wife and I started talking about having children. I thought it would be a good idea to start planning for the future of our family. I wanted to know more about saving and investing, so I took a CERTIFIED FINANCIAL PLAN-NER™ education program at the local university.

When I started the program, I was doing it merely for the benefit of my family, not for a career move. In fact, a few years earlier my wife, who is an accountant, had considered a career change to financial planning, but I had talked her out of it. I thought financial advisors were snake-oil salesmen—only interested in getting customers to buy a certain financial product.

However, while I was going through the program, I had a drastic shift in my mindset. I realized there are financial advisors who help clients achieve their goals and objectives without earning commissions on the types of stock they push. The professor who ran the program introduced me to this smaller subset of Fee-Only financial planners who work with a fiduciary mindset. Their sole interest is helping you get the most from your investments. Of the more than 300,000 people who called themselves a financial advisor, financial planner, investment advisor, or some other variation of those terms, there were less than 1 percent of advisors that adhered to a strict fiduciary oath and were members of the National Association of Personal Financial Advisors (NAPFA). Today, there are still only about 3,000 in the United States.

Contrary to popular belief, many advisors are not required to act in the best interests of their clients. If these advisors were interested in putting their client's interests ahead of their own, they would adhere to what is called the Fiduciary Standard of Care. While this may be a confusing and technical legal term, the definition of a fiduciary is anything but confusing: a fiduciary has a legal duty to act solely in the best interests of the client.

Sounds pretty good, right? It did to me, and that is why I decided to take that route in pursuing a career in financial planning. Once I completed the financial planning education program and left the navy, I worked for a Fee-Only firm in Chicago for about a year and a half before I struck out on my own more than sixteen years ago.

My wife, Laura, earned her MBA in finance and also became a CERTIFIED FINANCIAL PLANNER™ practitioner. She and I work together on the day-to-day activities of our company. We have three boys, from the sixth grade to a high school junior, and when I'm not at my desk, you can usually find me at soccer games or cross-country meets watching my kids.

WHY I WROTE THIS BOOK

When I started writing this book, people would ask me why I was doing it. There are multiple reasons.

First and foremost, I like to help people any way I can. Running a successful financial planning practice takes time, and there are only so many people I can effectively help each day. At times, I've had to turn away business because I was at full capacity working with my existing clients. Putting all of my recommendations into an easy-to-read book allows me to help more people than I could ever help in one-on-one financial planning engagements.

Additionally, some people merely need a little guidance on how to save and prepare for retirement. Maybe they don't need to engage with a financial planner just yet; they only need some actionable steps to take for a few years while building their retirement nest egg at the beginning of their careers. If you are in that situation, this book will help you.

Finally, one of my main goals in writing this book is to provide my current clients and potential clients with information in an efficient yet thorough way. When I meet with clients and we step through the financial planning process, it can often take months for us to go over all these concepts. This book will give my clients a reliable resource they can refer to whenever they wish. Potential clients can read this book and quickly get up to speed on my approach to financial planning and investing. This will help them grasp some of the concepts I recommend, and it will enable them to visualize the process I'll be going through.

For all of these reasons, writing a book seemed to be the right thing to do.

WHAT THIS BOOK IS AND ISN'T

I've been planning this book for years. After two decades of helping people, I have seen how fearful the process of retirement is for many. In some cases, my clients don't know if they've saved enough. In other cases, they aren't sure how to invest their savings so they can live off the earnings and not cut into the principal. Others are worried about how to properly organize their estate. I saw a need for a book that guided and reassured people as they planned for retirement.

What I've learned is that saving and investing for retirement isn't complicated, but it's not easy either. There are some basic building blocks to the process, and if you just assemble those blocks correctly, you can succeed. This book describes those building blocks and how to stack them up.

When it comes to retirement planning and investing, most of us know what we want but have no idea how to get there. Many simply do not know how to set themselves up for a safe and comfortable retirement. Society, government, and industry established this new system for retirement without training us properly and checking in from time to time to see how we're doing. Grade school, high school, and even college curricula don't prepare individuals with the basic knowledge or tools to plan for and achieve financial security in retirement.

When you read this book, I hope you feel like you're sitting down for an extended, relaxed conversation with a retirement planning and investment professional. I'm not here to criticize or judge you; I only want to share some ideas and offer some guidance. This book will help you understand how investments and the stock market work, but more importantly, it will take you on a journey through the steps necessary to build a comfortable retirement nest egg and to live off it long after you've stopped working.

Whether you are just starting in your career or have been saving for thirty years, this book will give you the information you need to navigate these choppy seas. Are you ready to set sail?

CHAPTER 1

THE REALITIES OF RETIREMENT

For many people, retirement is like a bear they've kept in the closet for many years. They know it's in there, but they don't want to think about it, and they certainly don't want to let it out and directly deal with it. Earlier in their life, the bear was just a cub—not much of a threat at all—but over the years, that bear has gotten bigger and nastier and hungrier, and by the time you let it out, you've got a big, snarling problem on your hands.

I understand why people are reluctant to deal with retirement. Earlier in their lives, when the bear was just a cub, people focused on other things, such as getting their careers launched and starting a family. It's not unusual for people in their mid-to-late fifties to reach a point in their lives where they've worked hard, paid off their house, and successfully put their children through college, and now they want to start focusing on their retirement. They've got five or ten years of work left, and they want to know what they can do to set themselves up for those years after they've left the workforce. They're finally ready to let the bear out.

Unfortunately, these folks needed to confront that bear much sooner in their lives. They can still save a lot of money in their remaining working years, but they've lost the decades of compounding financial growth they would have enjoyed if they'd only started saving earlier. That bear would have been so much easier to tame if its owners had spent more time with it when it was still a cub.

ARE YOU PREPARED?

We talked in the Introduction about how the retirement landscape has changed dramatically since the early 1980s. Pension plans are mainly a thing of the past, and people are now responsible for saving for their own retirement. Unfortunately, study after study shows they have not done a very good job.

Although many financial planners recommend that you have eight times your annual salary saved up by the time you're sixty (see "Savings Rates and You" sidebar), most people near retirement aren't even close to that figure. I read one study by the Economic Policy Institute that found that the median retirement savings for families between fifty and fifty-five years old is only $8,000. The median for families between fifty-six and sixty-one is only $17,000. One in three Americans have no retirement savings at all. Nearly 40 percent of the people the policy institute surveyed admitted that they had no plans to ever retire from work.

The problem doesn't seem to be getting better either. Millennials (people from seventeen to thirty-five years old) actually have less in their retirement accounts than the baby boomers (ages fifty-three to seventy-one) did at the same time in life. More than 40 percent of millennials haven't saved a dime for retirement, which is why I hope young people see this book and pick it up. They need to start saving now. Start now and don't stop, not even when faced with paying for your child's college education. I know millennials make less than baby boomers did at the same age, but they should still be trying to sock away 10 to 15 percent of their income. If you are making $50,000 a year, you can increase your retirement account by $100,000 over the next thirty years by increasing your savings from 4 percent to 6 percent. It might sting a little at first, but you'll get used to it.

I realize that these are sobering numbers. Part of the

reason they are so alarming is that people who are close to retirement age aren't taking into consideration how long they are likely to live. Thanks to advances in medicine and more focus on our personal health, the period between when you retire and when you die is much longer than it used to be. People retiring at fifty-five or sixty are often looking at a life span of another thirty years! That is a long time to stay in the workforce, and, if you retire, it's a long time to make your retirement savings last.

Most people focus on how much money they have saved for retirement without thinking about purchasing power. The greatest risk in retirement is the erosion of your purchasing power due to inflation. The price of gas and food is always going up, and you can expect it to double every twenty years or so. Remember the five-dollar lunch? Well, that's a thing of the past. People must take into account not only how long they are likely to live but also how much inflation is going to eat into their purchasing power.

If you're like most people, your retirement—from the day you retire until the day you die—will likely be split into three significant periods: the Go-Go Years, the Slow-Go Years, and the No-Go Years. Here's a chart I draw up for clients on the whiteboard in my office to explain this pattern.

SAVINGS RATES AND YOU

Your annual savings rate (including your employer's match) over your entire career should be more than 10 percent of your gross income. If you wait until you're thirty-two to start saving for retirement, you should save 10 to 15 percent of your gross income, and if you wait until you're in your late forties, you should save 15 to 20 percent of your gross income.

How do you know if you're on track to save enough? Here are some benchmarks for investment assets as a percentage of gross pay if you are working until full Social Security retirement age:

- **Age 25: 0.20 to 1** (this means you should save 20 percent of every dollar of income). In other words, if your annual salary is $50,000 at age 25, you should have $10,000 socked away for retirement by the end of that year.

- **Age 30: 0.6–0.8 to 1** (you should have 60 to 80 percent of your gross annual income saved for retirement).

- **Age 35: 1.6–1.8 to 1** (you should have 160 to 180 percent of your gross annual income saved for retirement).

- **Age 45: 3–4 to 1** (you should have 3 to 4 times your gross annual income saved for retirement).

- **Age 55: 8–10 to 1** (you should have 8 to 10 times your gross annual income saved for retirement).

- **Age 65: 16–20 to 1** (you should have 16 to 20 times your gross annual income saved for retirement).

RULES OF THUMB FOR OTHER CRITICAL FINANCIAL ISSUES

- Emergency savings: Three to six times your monthly expenses.

- Total debt payments should not exceed 36 percent of gross income.

- Consumer debt payments (credit cards, payday loans, auto loans) should not exceed 20 percent of gross income.

- Home mortgage principal, interest, taxes, and insurance should not exceed 28 percent of gross income.

- Debt-to-equity or total-liabilities-to-net-worth ratio at retirement should be 0 percent.

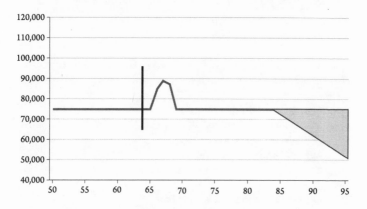

The vertical axis on the left measures how much money you're spending, and the horizontal axis across the bottom represents a person's age. The flat line leading up to retirement is a person's average annual spending level. The vertical black line in the middle is the year a person retires.

Typically, retirees continue spending at their preretirement levels for a short while before their spending goes up sharply for a few years. This is usually when a person or couple does some traveling or in some other way enjoys the good life. These are the Go-Go Years. The additional money they are spending might not go to travel but to other things, such as home improvements, a new golf club membership, or a workshop full of tools needed for a retirement hobby.

Whatever the case, the spending usually settles back to earth after the Go-Go Years. These are the Slow-Go Years, and your spending flattens out to where it was before retirement.

A person's later years—typically their early eighties—slide into their No-Go Years. This is when people slow down. They don't travel as much, and they don't go out much. Their spending declines. Their medical expenses often increase during this period, which is why I've added that shaded area. Even with insurance, your out-of-pocket costs at this life stage are likely to grow, so you have to plan for that as well.

HARDWIRED TO MAKE POOR DECISIONS

When looking at the realities of retirement, there's another factor to consider. Regardless of your age or stage in life, you are hardwired to make poor decisions in the stock market. What I mean is that all too often investors make emotional decisions about stocks and bonds that only serve to get them in trouble. For example, one of my clients decided to sell all of his stocks in 2009 when the economy was hitting bottom. For months, he had been watching his portfolio shrink as the economy contracted and people defaulted on their mortgages. The stock market lost enormous chunks of its overall value. Finally, my client couldn't take it anymore and began selling his stocks. I explained to him why this was a bad idea and that like all pullbacks in the stock market, this one too shall pass. When stock prices are low, you should invest, not divest! He likely would have regained most of his lost wealth over the next several months, but, after selling, his losses were permanent. This is what happens when we react and make emotional decisions.

Each year, Dalbar, Inc., a market research firm in Boston, releases its Qualitative Analysis of Investor Behavior, which examines investors' decisions to buy, sell, or switch out of mutual funds over the short and long terms. The goal of the study is to figure how to help independent investors avoid acting impetuously. Each year, Dalbar documents just how poorly investors do in comparison to the stock market in general. In 2016, for instance, the average equity mutual fund investor underperformed the S&P 500 by a margin of nearly 5 percent. While the market made close to 12 percent that year, the average equity investor earned a little over 7 percent.

There is nothing new about that kind of underperformance either. It happens routinely. In 2015, Dalbar looked at the twenty-year annualized return of the S&P 500 and compared it to the annualized return of the average investor for the same period. Guess what? The S&P return was 8.19 percent while the average mutual fund investor earned only 4.67 percent. Why are investors leaving so much money on the table?

The problem that I see and that Dalbar documents every year is the tendency among investors to choose investments that have done well in recent years. People just can't seem to help themselves. They are in a mutual fund that is doing OK, but then they notice this other mutual fund that is going gangbusters. Hey! Let's try that one out! The reason this strategy doesn't work is simple: the odds of a stock or mutual fund remaining at the top for an extended period is very slim.

Individual investors tend to chase investment returns like a slow game of whack-a-mole, always striking where the mole used to be but is no longer there. There is a reason that advertisements showing investment performance includes the ubiquitous disclaimer, "Past performance may not be indicative of future results." They are trying to tell you something! The SEC even has a rule that requires mutual funds to tell investors not to base their expectations of future results on past performance.

We'll get into this in more detail in chapter 5, when we talk about investing. However, for now, keep in mind as you ponder the realities of retirement what Dalbar tells us in boldface type: **do not chase yesterday's winners.** When you are retired and living off the growth of your nest egg, you will likely be paying closer attention to the stock market than you did in the past, and when you try to outguess the market, you will not do as well as you should.

THE EMOTIONS OF INVESTING

Over the last thirty years, many academic researchers have examined the behavior people exhibit when making economic decisions. In 2002, Princeton economist Daniel Kahneman won the Nobel Prize for his research on human judgment and decision-making during times of uncertainty. Kahneman and his fellow researcher, Amos Tversky, found that in these circumstances people don't always make rational decisions based on their self-interest. Instead, people frequently don't fully analyze situations that call for complex judgments.

Kahneman and Tversky's research inspired other researchers to apply cognitive psychology and human motivation insights to economic principles. Here are some of the key mistakes researchers have shown that people will make when managing their investments in retirement.

Overconfidence. When people see an investment pay off, they tend to believe they have an innate ability to read and anticipate the stock market. They think they have a knack for investing. This phenomenon is similar to what happens when you ask people about their driving abilities. Almost everyone will say they are a good driver—above average if not excellent. Well, everybody can't be above average, so maybe these folks are exaggerating their driving abilities. The same is true with investing. The best example is when the technology bubble burst in 2001–2003. Before that staggering downturn, most investors were overconfident and thought that tech stocks would continue to go up at the same rate they did in the past. These overconfident investors didn't have the historical perspective to realize that this particular stock market rally couldn't last. They lacked the healthy caution and skepticism that you need in the stock market. When you are overconfident in this way, you lose that sense of danger that forces you to look more carefully at what the future might hold.

Selective memory. People never tell you about the stock they lost money on, just the stock that made them a big profit. This unbalanced perspective leads many investors to believe that they are better investors than they are. Smart investors take the total picture into account, not just the benefits. When I was in the navy, we had to practice man-overboard drills. We did them all the time, and the reason for that is because in the event someone did fall overboard, we all knew exactly what we had to do to rescue that person. The same is true in the stock market. The market is going to drop—30, 40, or even 50 percent. Those kinds of drops are common. So do you know how you are going to react when that happens? You must always be prepared for how you are going to react in both good and bad times.

Confirmation bias. This occurs when people have some short-term success with a stock and become convinced that they should continue investing that way. There were, for example, many technology stocks that did very well in the late 1990s. But then the bubble burst. To this day, some investors want to put money into technology because they remember the meaningful gains they had before the tech bubble burst. They believe those stocks will rise again. This behavior is also called anchoring, because our first impressions hang with us, and we tend to ignore any information that does not support or line up with our ideas.

Regret aversion bias. A person's fear of regret can have a perilous effect on their investment decisions. Fear of regret can make you timid or it can make you more reckless. Here's how it works: say your brother-in-law pulls you aside to tell you about a large cap growth company he wants you to invest in. You buy the stock, but after three months, the stock value plummets, and you lose 50 percent of your initial investment. That stings, and you vow to thoroughly research any company your brother-in-law touts as a winner. By the same token, say you didn't invest and instead watched as your brother-in-law's tip went gangbusters and increased its stock value by 50 percent. You could have earned a bundle, and you regret *not* investing. The next time your brother-in-law recommends a stock, you jump on it. Either way, you are driven by regret—the regret about not vetting the loser and regret about not hopping on the winner. If you're prone to either type of that behavior, you need to take it into account when you're making future investment decisions.

Hindsight bias. This is when people think a major event, such as the Great Recession of 2008, was easily predictable. As they look back on it, the end result seems inevitable! Of course, we all could have seen it coming! This leads them to believe they can predict significant market shifts, and that results in overconfidence. As an investor, hindsight bias may allow you to think you don't need an objective analysis of a company before investing in it. Or that you can correctly buy or sell at the most opportune time. You should never make a sizable investment without first doing an objective analysis of the stock you're thinking about buying and whether it fits inside the portfolio you are developing.

Familiarity bias. I run into this with some of my clients in Cincinnati. General Electric and Procter & Gamble are both prominent companies in the area, and many of my clients' portfolios lean heavily toward P&G or GE. Investments in those companies paid off in the 1980s and 1990s, but in the last twenty years, they have been underperforming. Despite this, many of my clients are reluctant to sell their stock in those companies because they are familiar with them and trust them—even though a more diversified portfolio would have delivered better returns over the long term.

Self-attribution bias. This is when an investor believes that any success with a particular stock is directly attributable to the investor's skill and knowledge, and any losses are the result of bad luck, such as freak or unlikely events that were out of the investor's control. This leads to a dangerous level of overconfidence.

Trend chasing or herding. This is when investors notice that other investors are making money on a particular stock and feel a strong urge to invest in that stock, too. The problem with that kind of behavior is that the stock market often doesn't cooperate. By the time you notice the trend, it's probably over. Very few funds consistently stay at the top. According to the Dow Jones Persistence Scorecard, only about 6 percent of the 563 equity funds in the S&P 500 top quartile in 2015 were still in the top quartile the following year. This is why we diversify portfolios; when your stock in one company declines, your losses are counterbalanced because you also have shares in some other companies that may be rising.

Mental accounting bias. This is when you treat different pots of money differently. For instance, you have one portfolio that you reserve for conservative investments and another for high-risk investments. Each dollar in one account is equal to a dollar in another account, yet the investor treats them differently. The high-risk portfolio, in the investor's mind, is "play money"— somehow less valuable than the conservative portfolio funds. Some investors take it one step further and treat all gains as play money and invest those gains in high-risk, high-yield investments. This approach is not as lucrative as having a strategically balanced, diversified portfolio where every dollar counts. Mental accounting can hurt you in other ways, such as when you have a savings account, but also credit card debt. Instead of paying down your debt, you put money in a low-interest CD. The amount you owe is growing faster than what you are earning by saving, so it's illogical not to use the savings to pay off the credit card. Another way mental accounting bias hurts is when investors refuse to sell a certain profitable stock because they don't want to pay capital gains taxes. So they stick with the investment, even though a significant pullback could cost more than the capital gains would have.

Emotional decisions are a significant way people can lose money on their investments. Investors start out with optimism, and as their gains go up, they reach a state of euphoria. Then, as the market drops, anxiety, fear, and denial set in. In time, the investor is despondent over all his losses and decides he wasn't cut out for the roller-coaster ride and sells all his stocks.

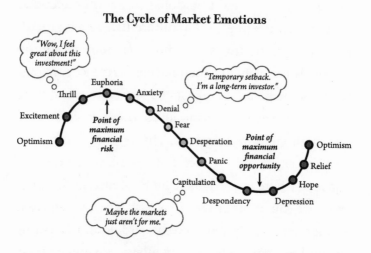

The Cycle of Market Emotions

That moment, when the stock market is at the bottom, and you're a basket case, is *the best time to invest.*

The opposite can also happen. Rising stocks make you feel euphoric and ready to invest more. However, that might be a good time to look somewhere else to invest. The point is that if you use your emotions to make investment decisions, you're probably doing the wrong thing at the wrong time. You're forcing yourself to buy high and sell low.

These are the kinds of decisions humans are prone to make. And these emotions can feel magnified in retirement. After you leave the workforce and are living off your investments, you need to be aware of all the behavioral mistakes that can cut into your portfolio. Most people, when they are working and putting money into their 401(k) accounts, don't pay much attention to the stock market. But when you retire, a 30 percent drop in the market can have a profound, emotional impact. This is one reason why many people who retire work with a financial planner; it gives them someone who can look at things and advise them without the heavy emotion that contributes to poor decisions.

These are some of the realities of retirement, but it doesn't mean you shouldn't let the bear out of the closet. So if you haven't already, let it out. Armed with the knowledge of how to avoid these common investment mistakes, you're almost ready to tame retirement. But before we start tackling some of the other issues posed by retirement, we'll have to take a look at your current financial situation. Read on so we can get a handle on your net worth.

Chapter 2

Start with Where You Are: An Analysis of Your Current Situation

A crucial step when you're deciding whether it's time to retire is to put together a one-page net-worth statement. This is typically one of the first things I do with my clients. The report has two columns of information: your assets on the left and your debts on the right. It's a simple document, although you might have to wade through a stack of bank statements, investment records, insurance policies, pay stubs, and other materials to get the numbers for it.

Here's what one looks like before it's filled in.

Net Worth Sample

ASSETS		
Liquid Assets		
Checking/Savings B of A		$
Business Account B of A		
Savings Account		
Brokerage Cash (Emergency)		
Total Liquid Assets		**$**
Investment Assets		
Revocable Trust Account	$ 100,000	$
Mutual Funds	10,000	
Co. Stock-ABC (1000@$20)	40,000	
Co. Stock-123 (125@$40)	10,000	
Stock Options		
Deferred Comp. Account		
Brokerage Account		
Cash Value Life Insurance		
Total Investment Assets		$
Retirement Assets		
Individual-1 IRAs		$
Individual-1 401K		
Individual-2 IRAs		
Individual-2 401K		
Total Retirement Assets		$
Total Investment and Retirement Assets		**$**
Business Assets		
Land		$
Business Investments		
Total Business Assets		**$**
Residence		
Value of Residence		**$**
Personal Assets		
Furnishings		$
Vehicles and Boats		
Jewelry		
Vacation Home		
Other		
Total Personal Assets		**$**
TOTAL ASSETS		**$**

(Investment Assets column labeled *Cost Basis*)

LIABILITIES	
Short-Term Obligations	
Consumer Credit Obligations	$
Borrowings on Life Insurance	
Installment Loans	
Personal Loans	
Accrued Income Taxes	
Other Short-Term Obligations	
Total Short-Term Obligations	**$**
Long-Term Obligations	
Loans	$
Mortgage (3.5% Var at 7/2030)	
Personal Vehicle Loans	
HELOC	
Total Long-Term Obligations	**$**
TOTAL LIABILITIES	**$**

NET WORTH | $

Assets not in Estate	
Asset 1	$
Asset 2	
Asset 3	
Asset 4	
Asset 5	
Asset 6	
Total Assets not in Estate	**$**

TOTAL LIABILITIES/ NET WORTH | $

People usually have a lot of these numbers floating around in their head—they know what their brokerage account has in it, for instance, and they have a rough idea of how much they still owe on their mortgage—but I have found that listing it all on one sheet of paper helps to put it in perspective.

This net-worth statement also provides valuable context. It shows how one area can affect another. For example, you might have $900,000 in your 401(k), but you still owe $215,000 on your house. You may have a modest savings account that you set up as a rainy day fund (or what we often call an emergency fund, which we'll discuss later in this chapter), while you're also carrying credit card debt that is costing you hundreds of dollars each year in interest payments. These types of conflicting financial situations will pop out when you do this net-worth statement and reveal areas that you might want to address before you retire. For instance, can you continue putting money in your company-match 401(k) while also making extra principal payments on your mortgage?

The net-worth statement is just a snapshot in time, of course, because your numbers will always be changing. But it's a vital picture because it shows where you still might need to do some work before you're ready to retire.

Here's a good example. I had one client come to me

when he was in his mid-fifties. He had a million dollars in his company 401(k), and he had decided he was ready to retire.

"A million dollars has been my bogey since I started working in the mid-eighties," he said. "Let's put it to work so I can retire."

The problem was that he was only looking at the asset side of things. As we discussed his future obligations, it came out that he was still paying on a couple of mortgages and that he wanted to cover his daughter's law school tuition. He also hadn't taken into consideration the cost of inflation. What's more, he needed to figure out how he was going to pay for healthcare. If he retired at fifty-five, he would need healthcare coverage for ten years before Medicare starts at age sixty-five.

He also hadn't fully thought through his retirement housing plan. He had a house in Southern California and some other properties in the Midwest, but he needed to lock down where he was going to live and how much that living arrangement was going to cost him. That, for any retiree, is an essential element of their retirement plan: where are you going to live and how much is that going to cost you?

Overall, he was in great shape on the savings side, but

when we factored in his short- and long-term obligations, the picture wasn't so rosy. His one-page net-worth statement made it clear where the soft spots were in his early retirement plan. Despite having a million dollars in his retirement account, the net-worth statement revealed that he couldn't retire at fifty-five and have enough money to pay for what could be a thirty-year retirement. Later in this chapter, I'll explain how my client addressed this situation.

PULLING THE INFORMATION TOGETHER

While it's important to collect all the information needed for your net-worth statement, keep in mind that the report is obsolete almost as soon as it's finished. The numbers will change depending on your savings rates, your investment returns, and your debt. Your loan balances will go down or disappear over time, for example, and we all know how stock prices can fluctuate and affect the asset side of things. As a result, your net worth is a moving target, although if you're investing wisely, there should not be any sharp downturns. So it's important to track it across time. I recommend updating it at least annually.

But knowing where you are right now—knowing what your debts amount to, how much you have in your emergency savings account, and the value of your assets— enables you to project into the future and have a better idea of what you need to do. If you are still ten or fifteen years away from retiring, your net-worth statement can be revealing. If, for instance, you still have twenty years left on your mortgage, you can quickly see how a house payment will eat into your retirement income. This can motivate you to set a goal of paying off the house in the next ten or fifteen years. And when you weigh that against your savings level, sometimes it jumps out at people that they really need to put their head down and do some catch-up so that they can be ready to retire when they want to. This is another real value of a net-worth statement.

When I meet with a client, I'll ask them to pull together the documents needed to prepare this net-worth statement. If you're not ready to work with a CERTIFIED FINANCIAL PLANNER™ practitioner, you can do it yourself. Here's what you need:

ASSETS

- All liquid assets, including:
  - Checking and savings account statements
  - Business account statements
  - Brokerage cash (emergency fund)
- Investment assets, including:
  - Revocable trust account statements
  - Mutual funds

- Company stock
- Stock options
- Deferred compensation accounts
- Brokerage accounts
- Cash value of life insurance
- Retirement Assets
  - A copy of your latest Social Security statement (go to www.ssa.gov/mystatement/ and open an account with Social Security to view your statement)
  - All IRAs and 401(k) accounts
- Business assets
  - Farm or timberland
  - Business investments
- Value of residence
- Personal assets
  - Furnishings
  - Vehicles and boats
  - Jewelry
  - Vacation home
- Wills, trusts, or other estate documents. This would include all durable powers of attorney for healthcare and property and living wills.
- Insurance statements for life insurance, long-term care, and disability insurance

LIABILITIES

- Short-term obligations
    - Consumer credit obligations
    - Borrowings on life insurance
    - Installment loans
    - Personal loans
    - Accrued income taxes
    - Other short-term commitments
- Long-term obligations
    - Farm loan
    - Mortgage
    - Personal vehicle loans
    - Home equity line of credit (HELOC)

It's a pretty long list, but keep in mind that these numbers are just a snapshot. They don't need to be accurate down to the last cent, and many of these figures change from month to month, if not day to day.

The value of the net-worth statement for someone planning their retirement is that the numbers can be projected into the future to reveal areas where you are behind. Say you're fifty years old and you are still fifteen years away from retirement. The net-worth statement can show at a glance how valuable it is, for instance, to pay off your car before you retire. People may not have considered that a crucial step toward retirement, but when you look at the net-worth statement, it becomes clear that they need to pay off that house before retiring. This might inspire someone to refinance to a fifteen-year loan or to make extra principal payments.

Many people create this net-worth statement on their own. They set up a spreadsheet with all the numbers and totals plugged in and then revisit it from time to time to update the numbers. It's an excellent tool.

A CERTIFIED FINANCIAL PLANNER™ practitioner can also help you with it. Occasionally, a new client will come to me with the net-worth statement already finished, and they are just looking for investment advice. That's fine, but people should be aware that a financial planner looks at the whole picture—your assets and investments along with your debts and future goals—before helping you design a plan. When calculating your net worth, your obligations are just as meaningful as your assets, and one affects the other. You can increase your wealth if you save more, but you can also increase your wealth by paying down your debts. If you're doing both simultaneously, you're moving toward retirement at a much faster clip. You really start seeing some great results.

A HYPOTHETICAL SCENARIO

Let's go back to the net-worth statement we showed you at the beginning of the chapter. This time, we'll add some numbers and explain what some of them mean. Here's what a typical net-worth statement looks like:

Net Worth Sample (David & Mary, March 2019)

ASSETS				LIABILITIES	
Liquid Assets				**Short-Term Obligations**	
Checking/Savings B of A			$ 1,000	Consumer Credit Obligations	$ 50,000
Business Account B of A			35,000	Borrowings on Life Insurance	–
Savings Account			25,000	Installment Loans	–
Brokerage Cash (Emergency)			–	Personal Loans	–
Total Liquid Assets			**$61,000**	Accrued Income Taxes	–
Investment Assets				Other Short-Term Obligations	–
Revocable Trust Account		$ 100,000	$ 150,000	**Total Short-Term Obligations**	**$50,000**
Mutual Funds	Cost Basis	10,000	15,000	**Long-Term Obligations**	
Co. Stock-ABC (1000@$20)	Cost Basis	40,000	20,000	Farm Loan	$ 40,000
Co. Stock-123 (125@$40)		10,000	5,000	Mortgage (3.5% Var at 7/2030)	200,000
Stock Options			25,000	Personal Vehicle Loans	25,000
Deferred Comp. Account			40,000	HELOC	50,000
Brokerage Account			40,000	**Total Long-Term Obligations**	**$315,000**
Cash Value Life Insurance			–	**TOTAL LIABILITIES**	**$365,000**
Total Investment Assets			**$295,000**		
Retirement Assets				**NET WORTH**	**$2,081,000**
David's IRAs			$ 100,000		
David's 401K			900,000	**Assets not in Estate**	
Mary's IRAs			50,000	College Savings (529 Account 1)	$ 22,000
Mary's 401K			250,000	College Savings (529 Account 2)	6,000
Total Retirement Assets			**$1,300,000**	College Savings (529 Account 3)	25,000
Total Investment and Retirement Assets			**$1,595,000**	College Savings (529 Account 4)	5,000
Business Assets				College Savings (529 Account 5)	15,000
Land			$ 100,000	College Savings (529 Account 6)	4,000
Business Investments			100,000	**Total Assets not in Estate**	**$77,000**
Total Business Assets			**$200,000**		
Residence				**TOTAL LIABILITIES/ NET WORTH**	17.5%
Value of Residence			**$450,000**		
Personal Assets					
Furnishings			$ 50,000		
Vehicles and Boats			40,000		
Jewelry			50,000		
Vacation Home			–		
Other			–		
Total Personal Assets			**$140,000**		
TOTAL ASSETS			**$2,446,000**		

- At the top of the Assets column, you would list all your liquid assets, including your emergency savings fund, which should include at least four months of your monthly household expenses. This money is not invested because you need to have it readily available and not subject to fluctuations in the stock market.
- The Investment Assets section is for your taxable investment accounts, and there could be several different types of accounts in here, or it could be limited to one well-diversified mutual fund. Retirement Assets include all your IRAs and 401(k) accounts. It's not uncommon for people to have a handful of these.
- Business Assets should include partnerships, farms, timberland, or inventory from a business. I typically list the value of your house as a separate item.
- Finally, you list any significant personal assets. These items—such as a boat or a collector vehicle—are valuable, but they don't help build your retirement paycheck unless you plan to sell them.

But as I have mentioned previously, your assets are just half the story. The right-hand column lists all your short-term and long-term liabilities. The top section captures all the loans and short-term debts you have, including credit card debt, personal loans, income taxes you've accrued, and any borrowings you've made against your life insurance. The second section reports your long-term debts, such as your mortgage, home equity loans, auto loans, and farm loans.

When I'm going through these debts with a client, we usually are talking about strategies for paying off at least these short-term debts. Having money in the bank is great, but getting rid of these short-term obligations and loans is even better. You can't ignore these numbers once they're on paper, so it's a good time to establish a plan for paying them off and improving your net worth.

At the bottom of the page, we divide your net worth (total assets minus total liabilities) and divide it by your total liabilities to calculate your debt-equity ratio. In this example, that ratio is 17.5 percent. The lower that number, the better, and a reasonable goal would be to get it to 0 percent before you retire.

The final section records any assets that are not part of your estate. The most common one I see are 529 accounts, which are tax-advantaged savings accounts for education expenses. Some people who have lived in many different states may have more than one account for each kid, and many retirees have also started 529 accounts for their grandchildren.

CASH FLOW STATEMENTS

The next step after compiling your net-worth statement is to create a cash flow statement. These statements are often detailed but are easy to put together. You list all your income sources and record your monthly and annual revenues for each. Then you list all your expenditures and record the monthly and yearly costs for each of those. In a third column, you list what percentage of your income is attributable to each item.

Here's an example of what one looks like:

Cash Flow Statement Sample
David & Mary, March 2019

	Monthly Amount	Annual Amount	% of Income
INCOME			
Wages, Salary	10,900	130,800	98.42%
Interest and Dividends	175	2,100	1.58%
Rent, Royalty, Partnerships	0	0	0.00%
Pension Income	0	0	0.00%
Social Security Income	0	0	0.00%
Total Income	**$11,075**	**$132,900**	**100.00%**
EXPENDITURES			
Income Tax (Federal & State)	2,800	33,600	25.28%
Property Tax	460	5520	4.15%
Residence Mortgage	1,300	15,600	11.74%
Investment Real Estate	0	0	0.00%
Life Insurance	100	1,200	0.90%
Homeowners Insurance	80	960	0.72%
Auto Insurance	130	1,560	1.17%
Medical & LTC Insurance	270	3,240	2.44%
Savings	500	6,000	4.51%
Charitable Contributions	100	1,200	0.90%
Medical Expenses	360	4,320	3.25%
Auto Operating/Maintenance	600	7,200	5.42%
Day Care	1,500	18,000	13.54%
Clothing	150	1,800	1.35%
Dining Out	150	1,800	1.35%
Dues/Subscriptions	30	360	0.27%
Education	500	6,000	4.51%
Entertainment/Recreation	50	600	0.45%
Gifts	175	2,100	1.58%
Groceries	400	4,800	3.61%
Household	300	3,600	2.71%
Gas/Water/Electric	175	2,100	1.58%
Phone	120	1,440	1.08%
Internet/Cable TV	55	660	0.50%
Security	65	780	0.59%
Travel/Vacation	125	1,500	1.13%
Other/Misc.	100	1,200	0.90%
Total Spending and Savings	**$10,595**	**$127,140**	**95.67%**
Cash Flow Excess (or Shortage)	**$480**	**$5,760**	

This sheet tells you how money is coming into the house and how it is leaving (and where it goes). It also reveals whether your income is sufficient to cover your expenses. I don't commonly go into this kind of detail with clients, but it does reveal to them whether they can meet their savings goals or whether they will have to make some adjustments to achieve those goals.

Say your goal is to save $500 a month for retirement. When you add that amount to your monthly expenditures, does it cause your expenditures to exceed your income? If so, you have to decide whether you are going to save less or cut some other expense to ensure you can make your savings goal. On the other hand, a cash flow statement could reveal that adding $500 to your savings doesn't put you in the red at the end of the month. When that happens, you may decide to increase the monthly savings amount immediately. It's important to note that any changes you make don't have to be permanent. You can continually adjust over time. I especially like to see when clients systematically increase their savings when they receive a new promotion, salary increase, or receive an unexpected bonus.

You can modify the sheet to your situation. For instance, if your income taxes are paid through your employer, you can just list your take-home pay as income and remove the income tax line from the spreadsheet. Likewise, your property taxes may be paid through your mortgage escrow account, so in those situations, you can just list your house payment and forget about property tax.

You want this cash flow statement to be simple but also comprehensive. If you're regularly paying a dog walker, house cleaner, or snow-removal service, make sure you account for those expenses in some kind of "Services" category.

The cash flow statement is useful to people who are trying to cut expenses and increase savings for retirement, but it's also useful when planning your retirement. When I meet with clients who are having trouble figuring out what their expenses will be in retirement, I'll pull out this list and say, "Out of these expenditures, which ones will still be around after you retire?"

In most situations, the big one is the mortgage payment. Paying off your mortgage before retirement brings you far-reaching benefits. Your property taxes will still be around, though, as will your homeowner's insurance and your utilities.

However, the amount you save, which can be significant, will likely decline after you retire. Some other expenses might also fall, depending on your retirement plans. You may not feel you need a housekeeper once a week, so you'll save money by having the cleaner come every other week. Your charitable donations may go down if you decide to volunteer your time rather than give cash donations. All of these changes can make a big difference. When they add up their expenses, most people are a little surprised at how long the list is. But it pays to spend a little bit of time calculating all these expenses so that you have the accurate numbers you need to make good decisions about how much to save and when to retire. For some people, the amount they are spending on certain things really jumps off the page at them. They'll say, "Wow, I didn't realize I was spending so much going out to eat," and they'll keep that in mind the next time they talk about whether to dine out or eat at home.

You may find that you'll have expenses in retirement that you didn't have when you were working, and it's important to consider those as well. Do you have grandchildren you are going to want to visit a few times a year? Do you have aging parents you'll need to take care of? We'll talk more about these types of obligations in the next chapter, but keep those unexpected expenses in mind when you are planning out your retirement cash flow.

You may also have other expenses you didn't anticipate. For instance, many don't realize that they are likely going to have to buy a car at some point after they retire because the car you're driving now won't last thirty years (the way you will). Another thing some people forget to budget for is the cost of a son's or daughter's wedding. The big day may not be on the horizon when you first retire, but when it rolls around, it is often a significant expense.

GETTING A CLEAR PICTURE

The point of all this is that to build a smart retirement plan, you must have a firm understanding of your current financial situation and your future prospects. If you're still ten or fifteen years away from retirement, use these numbers to focus your efforts over the next several years. You may be doing great saving for retirement, but your debts are an issue. Or, on the other hand, you've managed to keep your debts low and now it's time to ramp up your savings. In both cases, it's wise to tackle the issue from both sides—maintain your savings while reducing your debt. You should also be taking a hard look at your 401(k) account. If you're putting in only 6 percent because that is what your employer matches, you most likely need to find a way to increase your contributions.

In the case of my client who wanted to retire at fifty-five and live off the million dollars in his 401(k), he used the net-worth statement and the cash flow statement to determine that he needed to continue working for a few more years. Working longer allowed him to save more to help his daughter pay for law school. And even though his employer agreed to continue offering him medical insurance if he retired early, he decided to build a cushion into his savings to cover his healthcare costs if his employer cut his coverage before he qualified for Medicare.

In the end, he worked for another three years. During that time, he created a savings account to pay for his daughter's law school expenses, and he sold or paid off the properties he was still making payments on. Thanks to his net-worth statement, he could easily see where he was and where he needed to be before retiring. That net-worth statement allowed him to put some precise numbers on how much more money he needed before retiring, and that allowed him to set a firm date for his retirement. He wasn't guesstimating his future expenses and figuring he'd just work another five or ten years. He was able to narrow it down and retire as soon as possible.

A net-worth statement is valuable even if you are in your twenties or thirties and in the early stages of your career. Young people can have a lot of debt—such as student loans or a new mortgage—but they also have tremendous human capital. They are just entering their earning years, so they should have many years of increasing income to look forward to. Their net-worth statement is going to look a lot different than someone in their fifties, but they can still use it as a way of working toward retirement because they can track how their debts stack up to their savings and continue to make adjustments as they age.

GOOD MONEY HABITS

An accurate net-worth statement and cash flow statement inevitably reveal whether someone has good habits when it comes to money. Are you the kind of person who goes to the grocery store without a list just before dinner? If so, odds are you're going to come out with a lot of stuff that you don't need and a lot more stuff than the person who went into the store with a list and bought only what was on that list.

This is the analogy I use when I explain to clients why they need to develop good money habits. If you plan ahead, set specific savings goals, and determine ahead of time what you want to spend your money on, chances are you'll have a better net-worth statement when it comes time to retire. Here are some of the other money habits I encourage clients to have:

Pay yourself first. When we get paid, many of us pay our bills first, spend money on ourselves, and then save what's left over. Try reversing that process. When you get paid, save what you need to reach your financial goals, then pay your bills. Finally, see what's left over and decide whether you need that new, high-tech golf club or can get by for another year with your current one.

Pay down your high-interest debt. This should be a no-brainer, but how many of us make just the minimum payment on our credit cards? Spend some time to review your credit card bill; if you're being charged $50 a month in interest on a $1,700 balance, doesn't it make sense to make a concerted effort to pay down that debt? Paying off that credit card could have the added benefit of increasing your credit score, which could make future loans less expensive. You can also call your credit card company and ask for a lower rate, or transfer the balance to a low- or zero-interest card.

Track your spending. We've gone through how to set up a cash flow statement. Start one, and then track your actual expenses so you can keep a handle on where your money is going. If you're spending fifteen dollars a day on Starbucks and steak burritos from Chipotle, you might want to consider brown-bagging it more often. Set a strict budget and stick to it.

Make your goals specific and measurable. Create a five-year plan with specific goals for savings and debt reduction. There are even apps that can help you do this.

Follow the forty-eight-hour rule. This is when you're in the store and you see something you want but haven't saved or budgeted for it. Don't buy it. Leave the store and wait two full days. If it turns out you didn't need the item after all, great. But if you find you still need the item, set up a plan for saving to buy it, even if it means you have to bring homemade coffee to work in a thermos to save the money you usually spend at Starbucks.

Adopt personal spending rules. These are sometimes called heuristics, and they are just rule-of-thumb guidelines for spending money. For instance, you may have a rule that you and your spouse can't eat out more than twice a week, or that you will never spend over a hundred dollars on a pair of shoes. You probably already have a few of these guidelines built into your habits; the secret is to get specific about them and stick to them. In this way, informal rules become healthy habits.

Create an emergency fund. An emergency fund is your first line of defense when you face periods of reduced income or dramatically increased expenses. The rule of thumb for emergency savings is to have at least three months of your living expenses set aside, but I think that is insufficient and puts you on the edge. I advise my clients to keep five months' worth of expenses set aside. An emergency savings account can prevent you from dipping into your retirement savings when you hit a rough financial patch. Having an emergency fund to cover short-term expenses when you lose a job or face high medical expenses can also keep you out of debt and prevent other problems—such as low credit ratings—that can force you to pay higher interest rates in the future.

It's also important to make sure the funds are readily available. They can be in an interest-earning account, but they should not be invested in risky stocks or in an account that charges early withdrawal fees or other penalties. Savings accounts and certificates of deposits with short terms are often smart places to sock away your emergency money.

The need for some of these habits may become apparent when you do your net-worth statement and your cash flow statement. The importance of good spending habits becomes more paramount as we examine our next topic—retirement goals.

CHAPTER 3

IDENTIFY YOUR GOALS

Not everyone retires with a goal. Some people just want to sleep in, work in the garden, or volunteer at the library. They've had to set goals their entire professional life, and they are tired of it. They're through with goals, responsibilities, and deadlines.

When I broach the subject of retirement goals with clients, I stress the importance of having some kind of plan for *what* they want to do and *when* so we can put a price tag on it and plan for it. As Yogi Berra once said, "If you don't know where you're going, you'll probably end up someplace else."

Whether you are thirty and just opened your first IRA, or sixty and taking some long, hard looks at your savings, a retirement plan ensures you take the necessary steps to reach your goals.

Think of retirement as a vacation. That's not a hard thing to do, right? But what does that vacation look like for you, specifically? If I walk into a crowded room and say, "Hey, everybody, we're going on vacation," one person is going to think he's going to go hiking in the mountains, another person is going to picture a cruise ship, and someone else is going to pack for a few weeks on the beach in Mexico. Everyone has a different idea of what a vacation means, just as everyone has a different view of what retirement will be like. To properly plan your retirement, you need to have some specific goals.

SMART GOALS

When I talk with clients about their goals, many start talking about what they hope to do with their time. They say they want to take up woodworking or fly-fishing or work on their golf game.

Those are all great goals, but what I mean by goals is more about what your financial goals will look like. How much do you *need* each month (for nondiscretionary items such as utilities)? How much would you *like* to spend (for discretionary things such as travel)? How much do you want to leave for your children? Do you want to avoid having any type of job or obligation after you retire, or do you have a part-time gig in mind? These questions need to be addressed before you can develop a solid retirement plan.

I usually recommend that retirement goals be SMART—Specific, Measurable, Achievable, Reasonable, and Timely.

For example, we might dream of settling down in a well-appointed chateau in France for retirement, but that goal, though specific, may not be achievable or reasonable. However, your goal might be to travel or take a big international trip every year. That's also specific, possibly realistic, and timely as well. You can also quickly put a price tag on a goal like that by calculating the costs of airline tickets, lodging, tours, entertainment, and so forth. That makes it measurable. Great goal!

Some people have other goals. They want to enjoy the winter in Florida, for instance, or fly to the West Coast three times a year to help their daughter with her children. Another retirement goal might be to set aside enough money to put that grandchild through college. Rather than leave those goals to chance, it's better to plan for them and save money for them ahead of time.

It takes time and attention to detail to plan these retirement goals. Think about a pilot who is navigating from San Francisco to Hawaii. Throughout the trip, the pilot and copilot are continually adjusting their heading, because they know that being off by just a degree early on in the journey will leave them hundreds of miles from the airport in Honolulu.

The same is true for your retirement goals. If you can establish your destination ten, twenty, or thirty years before you retire, you are in a position to make minor adjustments that, if ignored, can leave you way off course or running out of gas over an empty ocean. Furthermore, if you wait too long to start identifying your retirement goals, you may find yourself well behind and be forced to make drastic changes to your lifestyle.

FINANCIAL PLANNING LIFE GOALS

If you surveyed thousands of people and asked them what their retirement goals are, seven things would drift to the top. I call them the seven wonderful wishes for a life well lived:

- Provide your family with a comfortable and safe home.
- Save enough to support and educate your children and grandchildren.
- Assist family members through their own life journeys.
- Raise responsible, productive, and happy children who contribute to society.
- Enjoy leisure time with your family.
- Have a stress-free, comfortable retirement with enough money to do what you want.
- Make a measurable difference in someone's life through charitable giving or work.

These are lofty aspirations, but most of them aren't exact or quantifiable. It's OK to strive for them, but it's also wise to identify specific, less philosophical objectives for retirement. If those ambitions are measurable and clearly defined, you can work toward them and feel assured that you can achieve them.

For example, if I have a client who comes in and says his goal is to retire to Florida, I'm going to want to know which part of Florida because homes in the middle of the state cost a lot less than those on the coast. The Gulf Coast? Sounds great. Let's sharpen the pencil and put some numbers down and see what's possible.

Concrete, achievable goals bring a great sense of comfort because you can say, "Yeah, that's something I can do. I can afford that." If one of your goals is to set aside $100,000 to pay for a grandchild's college education and you have to work a couple of extra years to make that happen, you enjoy a great sense of accomplishment when you make that goal. That is why I stress to my clients that they make SMART goals.

Many retirees find that they must take into account the cost and time involved in caring for aging parents. For some people, it means hiring a home health aide to drop in on their parents two or three times a week, or it might be as simple as checking on your folks yourself from time to time. Some people find they must see their parents every day, prepare their meals, do their laundry, and help them take their medication. If you have aging parents, think of the role you want to have with them.

Another factor to take into account is how much you want to contribute to your children's college educations. This is typically not an issue for people who are close to retirement because often their children have already finished college. However, if you're just getting started in your career, and you want to help pay for your child's college, you must plan for that at about the same time you are building your retirement savings.

One of the best options for college savings is to set up a 529 plan. A 529 plan is named after a section of the tax code, and it allows you to invest money without having to pay taxes on it—as long as the savings are used to pay for education expenses. What's more, other family members can also contribute to the fund, and the money can be spent on a variety of expenses, from tuition and books to room and board. The Tax Cuts and Jobs Act of 2017 increased the benefits of 529 savings plans. Previously, the plans could be used to pay for only post-secondary school expenses. Under the new law, the plans also can be used to pay for up to $10,000 of tuition annually for kindergarten through grade 12.

It pays to compare different 529 plans; some limit state income tax deductions, some charge more fees than others, and some offer matching grants. Evaluating the myriad of 529 plans that are available (every state sponsors one) is an area that a financial planner can add a lot of value. A financial planner understands the multiple variables and how those variables differ between 529 plans. Based on your specific circumstances, they can guide you to the best plan for you. Remember that the money you save is being invested by the fund operators, so make sure you're comfortable with the level of risk offered by the plan you choose.

While many of us dream of retirement, we should also try to identify our retirement plans as early as possible. When I'm working with young executives, we start talking about their retirement goals from the start. Retirement might still be twenty-five years away, but we put that target out there and talk about what we can do to reach that objective. That young executive is like the pilot headed for Hawaii, patiently and regularly recalculating his position and making minor course adjustments; a mistake at this part of the journey is going to lead to major course corrections in the end.

RETIREMENT PLANNING

When planning your retirement, it's vital to answer several questions as precisely as you can. These answers will help you and your financial planner identify any big goals so that you can start planning for them. Here's what I ask my clients:

What are your financial planning goals? Most answers to this question are broad and generic, but the question forces you to shift your thinking from *How much do I need to save?* to *What am I going to do with the money I've set aside?*

At what age do you want to retire? Give yourself two dates. The first one is the age it would be nice to retire and the second one is the age by which you feel you *must* retire. This answer makes your retirement more realistic in your mind and can be an impetus for making financial decisions based on that retirement date. For many people, it is not necessary to pick a specific date. Consider a few different dates and then play around with other factors— such as retirement benefits, taxes, and goals—to narrow down your choices. Choosing two retirement dates while holding all other variables constant allows you to quantify the trade-off in income during retirement. It becomes very clear to you when you can compare the differences between retiring at an earlier date compared to a higher monthly income associated with a later retirement date. After going through a few scenarios, an ideal retirement date eventually will emerge.

Do you plan to work part time in retirement? Some people intend to work during retirement whether they have to or not. It might be fun part-time work at the local golf course, or it might be a part-time version of the job you did before retiring. Either way, your choice can have a huge bearing on when you retire and how much you'll ultimately work in retirement.

How much do you want to spend in retirement? Many retirees don't know the answer, but it can prompt them to draw up a cash flow statement so they can figure it out. Once you have a complete cash flow statement, it's much easier to determine what your spending will likely be in retirement.

Are you anticipating any sizable expenses before retirement? This, too, could have a considerable impact on when you retire. How do you plan to finance the expenditure? How will payments on that expense affect your cash flow?

Are you anticipating any significant expenses within the first five years of retirement? While many of us can't foresee a car breaking down and other expenses, others already know what's coming down the pike—a new roof, a house renovation, or some kind of extensive trip. Others anticipate helping a child or grandchild with college expenses. Parents could be expecting to pay for an expensive wedding for their son or daughter. Many of these expenses can be quantified, which makes them easier to plan.

Are you planning to change your housing after retirement? If you're planning to downsize or move to a warmer climate, a financial planner will want to get as much detail as possible. Any changes in your housing expenses would have an impact on your net-worth statement and possibly the timing of your retirement.

Do you plan to care for an aging parent or a disabled child in retirement? These types of expenses could dramatically affect both your cash flow and your net worth. A financial planner can help you prepare for this so the costs are more manageable.

Do you anticipate receiving an inheritance? How much? Some people have an idea of an inheritance that might be coming their way, but most won't. Either way, it's usually my recommendation to be conservative and not count on these funds when planning for your retirement.

How much cash on hand to you feel you'll need for emergencies? We'll talk more about the importance of a three-to-six-month emergency cash fund in a later chapter, but it's vital that you set these funds aside for a time when you need them.

Do you plan to make any sizable gifts or donations after retirement? Many parents have a goal of living off the proceeds of their savings so they can give the principal to their children. Others have a strong charitable intent and want to leave a legacy for a nonprofit that is close to their heart. Either way, it's important to have a clear idea of what you want.

It would be great to have answers to all of these questions. However, there is one very important thing to keep in mind: if you are in a long-term relationship with someone whom you plan to spend your retirement years with, it is vital that you discuss these questions and agree on what *both* of your goals are.

IT'S A VACATION

Remember, it helps to plan retirement the same way you would plan a vacation. What does vacation look like to you? Be specific. Where are you going? Are you driving or flying? How much will it cost? Where are you staying? What do you want to do when you get there? Is that activity an extra expense or part of the package? Without answers and a quantifiable plan, you may know what airport you're leaving from, but you won't know where you are going or how long you're staying there.

Your answers to these vacation/retirement questions will

be dictated by your retirement savings, so it's best to plan early. Make a plan and then start saving for it. It's never too soon.

It's also never too late. If you're in your fifties and approaching retirement, your choices may not be as broad as they were when you were younger, but you can still put a price tag on your ambitions and start working toward achieving them. After all, if you don't know where you're going, you'll never know you've arrived.

However, even the best-laid plans can go awry. Read on to find out how to protect yourself from major threats that could derail your retirement plan.

CHAPTER 4

INSURANCE: PLANNING FOR CATASTROPHE

WHY YOU NEED LIFE INSURANCE

As a Fee-Only financial planner, I'm not in the business of selling life insurance. But it's my responsibility to look at your financial needs and goals in a holistic way, so when an impartial trusted advisor looks at your situation in that light, life insurance still makes sound financial sense.

When I talk to clients about their life insurance needs as they plan for retirement, I often begin by drawing a graph on the whiteboard. The vertical axis shows how much life insurance you need and the horizontal axis shows your age. The red line in the middle represents how much coverage you need at various stages in your life.

Here's what that chart looks like:

Typical Life Insurance Need

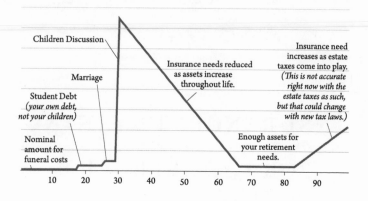

You have very little need for life insurance when you're an adolescent or teenager, so the red line starts out flat and near zero. The only financial needs you will have at this time are your final expenses. The first bump comes when you take out student loans for college, and the second bump occurs when you get married. At this point in your life, you have some obligations. You want to have a policy that will pay off those loans if you die (so your spouse, or cosigners, or parents won't have to) and you want to leave something to help your widowed spouse get back on his or her feet after your death.

The next increase is a bit more than a bump. It's more like a mountain—along the lines of those sudden, steep, and towering mountains like the Rockies or the Sierra Nevada that suddenly jut up from the plains. It comes when you and your spouse start talking about children.

Notice that I didn't say this dramatic jump in your insurance needs comes when you *have* children, but when you *start talking about* having children. If it's a serious conversation, you need to go out and get your insurance right away. Here's why: every day you're not covered with life insurance is another day that you could become uninsurable to a life insurance company. The longer you wait, the higher the risk that you'll be diagnosed with diabetes or some other problem that makes you undesirable to insurance companies. The earlier, younger, and healthier you are, the easier and cheaper it is to get a life insurance policy. This is why some people recommend buying life insurance as early as possible, even before some of these life events happen to you.

Here's another reason. Typically, at this stage in life when you and your spouse are talking seriously about having children, you are also likely to be at a point when your financial capital is low, but your human capital is high. Remember, human capital refers to your potential future earnings. You've been through school and started your career, but you haven't socked a lot away in terms of savings, or home equity, or other assets at this stage. You have great earning potential, and life insurance helps you protect and ensure the wealth you are on the verge of producing. In this sense, you are already using life insurance to prepare for your retirement. Life insurance is there to replace the earnings stream (monthly salary) that your dependents rely on and that would be permanently interrupted if you were to die prematurely.

As you're working, saving, and investing, your liabilities shrink, your assets grow, and your need for life insurance trails off. This is not true for everyone, of course, but if you follow the typical pattern, your ratio of assets to liabilities decreases as you age. When that ratio reaches zero—the flat line on the right side of the graph—you can usually stop buying life insurance.

This graph shows a sharp increase in life insurance needs for people in their eighties. This was the case years ago when estates were taxed at a 50 percent rate for estates over $675,000. People were turning over a lot of their wealth to the federal government, and insurance companies sold policies to help people recover some of that money. Nowadays, estate taxes don't kick in until the estate is more than $20 million, so this spike in insurance needs is outdated. Nevertheless, tax law could change at any time, so we've left that spike in there to remind people that their life insurance needs *can* change later in life.

LIFE INSURANCE AS YOU AGE AND BUILD WEALTH

Although your need for life insurance declines as you get older and accumulate wealth—because you can use your wealth to pay for things you once needed life insurance to cover—I still recommend my clients carry it until they retire or even into retirement. Here's why:

- If you still carry a mortgage, life insurance payouts could help your spouse pay off the loan in the event you die. Even if you miss out on retirement by passing away young, you still wouldn't want your spouse to be forced to sell the family home because he or she couldn't make the payment without you.
- If you intend to help your children through college, either by paying for it entirely or by cosigning for their student loans, a life insurance policy will help cover that obligation if you pass away.
- You may have a responsibility to care for older family members. If you do, and you die before you've carried out that obligation, a life insurance policy will help you meet those obligations.
- If there is a special-needs situation in your family, or if you have a dependent who has special physical or mental disabilities and would rely on your income to continue a level of care or support, funding that need after your death could be accomplished by a separate pool of insurance proceeds earmarked for that special situation.

- You may want to provide a legacy for future grand-children.
- Both spouses, regardless of whether both work, should be covered. If the stay-at-home spouse who cares for your children dies, a life insurance policy will help the surviving spouse manage the costly challenge of day care.

For these and other reasons, I don't recommend that clients cancel their life insurance policies. Chances are they signed up for the policy when they were young and premiums were low, so it makes sense to keep paying until the term has expired.

TYPES OF LIFE INSURANCE TO CONSIDER

Life insurance is a way for you to protect your loved ones in the event of a catastrophe. By catastrophe, I don't mean a hurricane, or wildfire, or an earthquake that wipes out your home and destroys all of your possessions. Those are tragic occurrences, but life insurance doesn't help you recover from them. The kind of catastrophe I'm talking about is when you you are killed in an auto accident. If you're young and just getting started, you haven't been able to convert your human capital into financial assets that will take care of your spouse, children, and financial obligations.

Insurance can be confusing because of all the different products created by life insurance companies. I've highlighted the different types below. If you have any questions, many independent experts have published articles online that explain the pros and cons of different policies, and these reviews will likely help you more than an insurance agent who is financially incentivized to convince you to buy a particular product.

The two main types of life insurance policies are term life and permanent life insurance. While the differences are clear regarding the amount of time you are covered by these insurance policies, one little-known difference is that permanent life insurance has a cash value component to it.

Cash value life insurance comes with an investment-like component that gains value over the life of the policy. Owners can also borrow against the cash value like a loan, and the cash value is paid out upon the policyholder's death.

Life insurance policies that have a cash value include whole life and universal life.

WHOLE LIFE INSURANCE

A whole life insurance policy is guaranteed to remain in force for your entire lifetime, provided premiums are paid throughout the contract. Additionally, whole life offers a guaranteed cash value growth and dividends. You normally pay premiums until death, except for some limited pay policy options, which may be paid up in ten years, twenty years, or at age sixty-five.

Because whole life policies are in force for such a long time, the premiums are typically much higher than those of term life insurance. I've seen whole life policy premiums that were nearly ten times higher than term life premiums for the same amount of coverage.

Some whole life policies come with an investment wrapper. In addition to the death benefit, they have a savings and investment component that allows you to accrue interest and dividends that you can then reinvest in the policy. You can also borrow against the cash value—provided you've been able to put money into the account over and above your premium payment—or withdraw funds if you have any equity.

Many people find they get better returns on their investments by buying term life insurance and investing in the stock market instead of investing in a whole life policy. Permanent life insurance's growth rate is often much less than what you make with mutual funds and exchange-traded funds.

UNIVERSAL LIFE

Universal life insurance is another type of cash value life insurance. In these policies, the excess of premium payments above the cost of insurance is credited to the cash value of the policy. The policy is charged each month by a cost of insurance (COI) along with many other policy charges and fees that are drawn from the cash value. An interest rate is used to credit the account, and there is usually a contractual minimum rate (often 2 percent).

When an earnings rate is pegged to a financial index, such as a stock, bond, or other interest-rate index, the policy becomes an Indexed Universal Life policy. Such policies offer the advantage of guaranteed level premiums throughout the insured's lifetime, but the cost of insurance will start low and gradually increase as you age. The result is that it has a substantially lower premium cost than an equivalent whole life policy in the beginning years.

Universal life doesn't have the guaranteed level premium that's available with whole life policies. Variable rates also mean the interest on the cash value could be low. Furthermore, a policy usually needs to have positive cash value to remain active. So if there is not enough cash, the policy will lapse, and it will prevent you from being able to take loans against the cash value.

VARIABLE UNIVERSAL

Variable universal life insurance (often shortened to VUL) is a type of universal life insurance that usually builds a cash value because it can be invested in a wide variety of separate investment accounts, similar to mutual funds. The choice for where to invest the money is entirely up to the contract owner and it often is like a 401(k) plan where you have a limited number of investments to choose from. The "variable" component in the name refers to how those separate accounts will perform over time, just like the stock or bond markets. If you pick the right investments, your account can grow quicker. This is a key advantage of VUL over whole life. With a whole life policy, the death benefit is limited to the face amount.

As with most complex insurance products, the fees and expenses can be very high, so examine those carefully before purchasing. Also, be forewarned about the projections that are used to sell these products. These projections are just that, "projections on a possible scenario that could happen." However, many times the projections are based on too rosy of a picture and can be highly unlikely to occur. It is in these situations that the term *buyer beware* needs to be at the top of your mind. Critics say insurance salespeople can make more in one year selling you the wrong policy than they will in ten years selling you what you need.

TERM LIFE

Term life insurance policies are more straightforward and cheaper, and I typically recommend them for my clients. With term life, the only value is the guaranteed death benefit. When the term expires, you can either renew (at a recalculated premium based on your age, sex, and possibly health) or just let the policy lapse. If you die after the term expires, there is no payout.

The idea of paying premiums and never receiving a benefit annoys some people, but you have to keep in mind the purpose of the product: to take care of your loved ones if you die and are no longer the breadwinner for the family. How will they make the house payment? How about the car payment, or the kids' college funds? If your spouse has to go back to work, who is going to pick up the kids after school? If something happens so you can't transition your human capital into financial capital, that's where insurance steps in.

How much life insurance do you need? That varies over time and from family to family. A good CERTIFIED FINANCIAL PLANNER™ professional can walk you through all the considerations you need to make. You must take into account how much you earn, how much you owe, how many years until retirement, and how much your assets are worth. If you have plenty of assets, do you really need life insurance? If you are twenty years from retirement, just hit the lottery, and have a bunch of stock options, I don't believe you need term life insurance.

The most significant expense items in many families, as we've mentioned, are mortgage and college. If you still owe a lot on your house and if you plan to pay for your kids' college, get enough life insurance to cover those big-ticket items. On the other hand, if you are merely cosigning the loans a child is using to pay for college, law school, or medical school, it makes sense to get a life insurance policy on your child. If you cosign a loan and something happens to your son or daughter before those loans are paid off, you could be facing a bill for $100,000 or $150,000. An insurance policy eases that burden.

A term life insurance policy for a young person is usually very cheap because the odds of needing the policy at a young age are very low. While the probabilities of needing a policy like that are minimal, there is some risk. If you want to take that risk, that's fine. However, most of the time when I have a conversation about insurance needs with clients who have cosigned for significant student loans, they run out the door and get a policy on their child.

WHAT ABOUT AN UMBRELLA POLICY?

While you might not need a life insurance policy after you

retire, I often recommend that my clients get an umbrella policy—particularly if they have a sizable net worth.

An umbrella policy is extra liability insurance designed to protect you from sizable claims and lawsuits in the event you make a mistake and cause an accident while driving, or someone gets hurt at your home. It protects your assets and your future. It's usually an extra layer of protection added to your homeowners and auto insurance. Because it puts your insurance company on the hook for a potentially significant payout, it incentivizes the company to step in and represent you in the event you have an accident.

If you are at fault in an accident that kills someone—such as a young professional who is just starting a family and just beginning to convert their human capital into financial capital—the claim against you could be significant. If you have substantial assets that you want to protect— your home, for instance, and all your savings—then an umbrella policy that covers your net worth makes a lot of sense.

Most companies won't write an umbrella policy for less than $1 million. The minimum amount of umbrella coverage should at least match your net worth. An umbrella policy can also cause your auto and homeowner's coverages to increase because of how insurance companies underwrite their policies.

LONG-TERM DISABILITY INSURANCE

Most people don't think about disability insurance. They might think Social Security will help them if a serious illness or injury forces them out of the workforce. However, it's difficult to qualify for these benefits, and often the payments are below what you'd need to cover your expenses.

Most disability insurance policies cover just 60 percent of your pre-disability income. Most of us would struggle to take a 40 percent pay cut and not have to make drastic changes to our living habits. It's worse if you're a younger person who has few assets or savings. Disability benefits are not indexed for inflation, so if you're thirty-five years old and you become disabled, you are looking at a thirty-year period where you can make only 60 percent of the salary you made in the early stages of your career. We know expenses usually double about every twenty years, so if your annual disability payment is $60,000 at the age of thirty-five, due to the impact of inflation that payment would have the purchasing power equivalent to $20,000–$25,000 by the time you're sixty-five.

An own-occupation policy is better than an any-occupation policy. An own-occupation policy is more expensive, but if you're a college professor and an accident prevents you from teaching, an own-occupation disability insurance will replace a more significant portion of your lost salary than an any-occupation policy.

Despite the overall limitations, I recommend disability insurance to my clients. Not every client I meet with walks out the door convinced they need it, however. Some just say, "Nope, I'm just going to take the risk. I don't want to buy another insurance policy." One crucial factor is that disability insurance usually stops at age sixty-five, so those approaching that age don't have a lot of years at risk.

WHAT ABOUT A POLICY TO COVER YOUR PENSION?

Although most retirees don't need cheap term life insurance, I sometimes recommend life insurance for clients who rely on one spouse's pension to fund their retirement.

In many cases, if the husband or wife receiving the pension dies early, the surviving spouse will receive only 50 percent of their partner's benefits. But half of a pension is rarely enough to cover the lifetime of the surviving spouse, so it makes sense in these cases to have life insurance for the first ten to twenty years of the pension.

For many pension plans, when it comes time to retire, you are given some choices for survivor benefits (i.e., 0 percent, 25 percent, 50 percent, 75 percent, or 100 percent). You should look at the differences in payout as being the cost of insurance to cover that amount for the surviving spouse. It then becomes fairly easy to see if the reduced benefits cost more or less than the equivalent life insurance costs. Any time the survivor benefit option chosen is less than 50 percent, the spouse must sign an acknowledgment that they are giving up their benefit rights. Most companies require that signature to be notarized. If you consider taking less than a 50 percent survivor option, take your time and ensure it's the right path.

I had one client who ran the numbers and realized that it was smarter for him to take the 100 percent option on his pension. He got 100 percent of his pension, but if he died, his wife would get nothing. However, he bought a life insurance policy with his extra pension money. He died in his mid-sixties, but his wife's needs were covered through insurance even though she didn't receive any pension payments.

DO YOU NEED LONG-TERM CARE INSURANCE?

According to the federal government, 40 percent of all long-term care recipients in the United States are under the age of sixty-five. Among those older than sixty-five, about 40 percent will spend some time in a nursing home and 70 percent will need some form of long-term care in their life. And the cost of this care, which varies depending on what part of the country you live in, can be high. The average cost of a nursing home is $225 a day, or about $82,000 a year.

Most can't look to the government for help. Medicare

might contribute to the first hundred days you stay in a nursing home, but there are no benefits for intermediate-term or custodial care unless the state finds the patient to be impoverished.

This is why some people carry long-term care insurance. If they have to move into a nursing home, these policy-holders won't have to drain their retirement savings to pay for care because their long-term care insurance will cover the costs.

Some people plan for long-term care by building up their net worth and assets so they can pay for the care when the need arises. In a sense, it's like life insurance; some people self-insure themselves against long-term care costs instead of buying a policy. They know that even if they go into a nursing home, they will not be impoverishing their spouse or their children because they have the assets to cover the bill.

When you look at the staggering costs of long-term care, you can understand why some people opt for this type of insurance. However, a lot of companies are getting out of the business of providing those types of policies because it hasn't been as profitable for them as they hoped when they started thirty years ago. Every situation is different, but if you have a long-term care policy from many years ago, you should take comfort in knowing you probably have a policy that will work out better for you than it does for the insurance company.

The sweet spot for signing up for this kind of coverage is when you are from fifty-two to fifty-five years old. Waiting until then means you can avoid paying premiums when you're younger and unlikely to need the care. But waiting until your mid-fifties puts you at risk of not being able to get a policy at all, or it may come at a very high cost. You may also need to shop around to find a policy that meets your needs. Like certain types of life insurance, these policies can come with all sorts of bells and whistles. How many years of coverage do you want? Do you want compounding or straight inflation? Do you want dual coverage for both you and your spouse? How long are you willing to wait until the benefits start—60, 90, or 180 days?

In deciding on whether this kind of policy is right for you, you have to go back to our original discussion about catastrophes. Is it a catastrophe if you have to pay long-term care for someone for three or six months? For most people, that would not equate to a full-blown catastrophe. It might hurt, and it might be a lot of money, but you can cover it. However, is it a catastrophe if your spouse is diagnosed with Alzheimer's and is going to have to be in a nursing home for the next eight to ten years?

In my mind, yes, that's a catastrophe. You should take actions to be prepared for it, and long-term care is an easy solution if you don't have the assets to cover those needs.

Chapter 5

Investing Basics

Now that we have talked about some of the foundational aspects of financial planning, it's time to move on to the topic of investing. Most people think retirement planning starts here, but I tell my clients that I can't begin to build an investment portfolio for them until I know what their retirement goals are and how well they have saved up to this point in their lives. That information drives a lot of the investment decisions we need to make. Having done that in the last few chapters, let's dig into investments.

Many people who are close to retirement have different ideas about what investing means. Some picture buying a business, such as a mini storage facility that provides a steady income. Others think purchasing rental real estate might make a lot of sense. These folks aren't opposed to investing in the stock market, but they might worry about the market's volatility. Wouldn't buying rental properties be a safer investment than the stock market and provide more reliable income for their retirement?

Not necessarily.

While rental properties or some other small business can provide a reliable, passive income, the truth is that you will still need to be involved in the day-to-day management of that investment. You must find tenants, fix the property, advertise vacancies, conduct background checks, and pay for insurance. You are running a small business, and many retirees don't want to work that hard.

However, with the stock market, you can still reap the rewards without having to be involved in the work and management of the business. When you invest in successful companies by buying stock in those companies, you benefit from the labor of all the people who work for that company. Those people go to work every day focused on selling more products or developing innovative new products. As a shareholder, you profit without lifting a finger. Your role is to find a company that is on its way to fresh profits or continued prosperity.

It's easy for me to explain the advantages of the stock market once clients know some facts about investing. For instance, did you know the following?

- Stocks are a simple and easy way for you to participate in the growth of great companies throughout the world and create wealth for you and your family.
- Stocks offer exceptional potential for growth, and US stocks have consistently earned more than other investments over the long term, despite their regular ups and downs.
- Investing in the stock market is the only way most people have of building real wealth throughout their lives. On average, large cap US stocks have returned over 10 percent since 1926 and small cap stocks have done even better. Factor inflation into this equation and you can receive returns that are two to three times above the increases in your expenses.
- The single most important reason to start investing right now is because you will be participating in the "greatest mathematical discovery of all time" according to Albert Einstein—compound interest! Through the miracle of compounding, your gains begin to earn money, and then those gains you make every year also earn money. Over a long time, your results increase exponentially.

I don't receive any benefit for recommending certain types of investments to the clients I work with. I just know that stocks are one of the simplest ways to help you prepare for and live through thirty-plus years of retirement. Whether you're just starting or have been saving all your life, a globally diversified portfolio should be the basic building blocks of your retirement plan.

WHAT YOU CAN CONTROL AND WHAT YOU CAN'T

When I am talking to people about investing, I talk about what you can control and what you can't control. You can't control volatility in the stock market, and you can't control what future returns will be for different asset classes. As a result, I try to explain that my role is to identify and manage those variables that we can control. These include:

1. The appropriate mix of stocks and bonds for each investor's goals and risk tolerance
2. Taxes
3. Expenses of investment products
4. Level of diversification
5. Tax efficiency of investments

When you put them all together, you start to understand there is a whole lot more to saving and investing than what you hear every day on CNBC. Spending your time focused on the above items will lead to a much better investing experience.

HOW I CHOOSE INVESTMENTS

I'm often asked how I choose the investments we use in client portfolios. To me, it is a process of multiple decisions that ultimately leads to the final selection. It's very important to have a well-thought-out process before you start looking for where to invest your money. If your only desire is to find the best performing mutual fund in advance every year, you may be setting yourself up for failure. As Jason Zweig has said in the *Wall Street Journal*, "When you chase outperformance, you catch underperformance."

The questions at the beginning of the process seem to be very broad and general, but they are anything but. The first major decisions you make will have the largest impact on how a portfolio returns over the long run. The big choices of how much do we want in stocks, bonds, and cash will far outweigh the impacts of choosing mutual fund A versus mutual fund B.

It's important to have an overall philosophy of how to invest. My philosophy can be boiled down to the following major areas:

- We should diversify systematically across the broad spectrum of stock investments. Individual companies can (and do) go out of business regularly, so this translates to being invested in large and small cap stocks and international stocks and making sure we are capturing the returns of both value and growth stocks.

- I focus my attention on Nobel-Prize winning academic research. I typically ignore marketing research because there is usually a large amount of data mining or other biases that skews the results of those studies. It's just like a car salesman who highlights the positive aspects of a car and minimizes its negative aspects. It's crucial that investors know where the "facts" are coming from.

- I keep a sharp eye on expenses by holding lower-than-average-cost investments and emphasizing after-tax returns. The investments should minimize taxes and the turnover of the fund's holdings should be lower than average. Having low expenses and transaction costs is like running a race where one person has six-inch hurdles (low fees) while someone else has three-foot hurdles (higher fees). These factors can be determined before the race starts.

- Expenses reduce investment returns. The costs of active management can create a handicap for active investors in the range of 2.5 percent to 9 percent per year, depending on asset class mix and whether a salesperson is involved. The least expensive form of active management, no-load mutual funds and "wrap fee" accounts, can also consume more than 2.5 percent per year from investors' returns.

- Because active portfolio managers are susceptible

to style drift—a commonly observed trait of skewing a portfolio's asset allocation to chase recent high performance of specific securities—my company primarily employs structured, institutional asset-class pooled accounts, exchange-traded funds, and fixed-income securities to fund your portfolios. These types of investments have a strict adherence to their asset class.

- I expect to own an investment for a very long time. Warren Buffett likes to say that when investors make a decision to purchase part of a company, you should do so with the expectation that you are going to hold the investment forever. There are no shortcuts to investing in the stock market.
- I like to ensure the mutual fund company or other investment products are suitable for each client and that the company we are investing in is going to be faithful stewards of our investment.

Many people think of the stock market as a get-rich-quick scheme where they can discover the next Microsoft. They think, "If I can find the right company to invest in, I'll be a millionaire in ten years!"

That's not the type of investing I talk about with my clients or the behavior I try to encourage. I emphasize maintaining a pool of assets that enables my clients to achieve their long-term financial goals. These assets can be developed into a stream of income that helps them meet their spending needs in retirement and ensures they leave a legacy for their children and grandchildren. The stock market can create an overnight millionaire from time to time, but that is rare. It's much more reasonable to view the stock market and your portfolio as a way to accrue a stream of profits that meet your needs when you leave the workforce.

THE DIVERSIFICATION KEY

To achieve that income stream, I advocate a diversified portfolio and investing in a way that minimizes your fees and expenses. Investing should not be the heart-pumping, risk-taking endeavor that's often portrayed on television and in movies. The great economist Paul Samuelson once said that sound investing should be as exciting as watching paint dry. I like to say investing in the stock market is like watching an oak tree grow.

Although I believe investing should be a patient and methodical process, I do sometimes compare investing in the stock market to a roller-coaster ride. I make that comparison not because I think of stock market investing as a thrill ride, but because I want my clients to understand this point: you never see people jumping out of a roller coaster in the middle of a ride. Once people get in, they should stay locked in to be safe. They should be content to stick it out for the entire trip so that they can get out safely in the end. Choosing to get off the roller coaster at the scariest possible moment—like bailing out of a solid long-term investment because the stock price temporarily went down—is not a wise course of action. You have to ride those dips out, and many times, it makes sense to find a way to invest more money during those dips.

As I discussed in chapter 1, for some reason, people are hardwired to do the wrong thing at the wrong time. I've already mentioned one client who decided to pull out of the stock market in 2009 when the market was taking a nosedive. The S&P 500 had lost about half its value. My client could see his portfolio value shrinking, but I recommended he ride it out. Well, I did more than recommend. I pleaded with him: hold firm; this too shall pass.

Still, this client couldn't bear the losses and sold out. He sustained losses that he could never recover because as the stock market came back, he no longer had the shares he needed to profit from as those share prices climbed back up. In truth, rather than *selling* shares in 2009, he should have been *buying* shares.

WHAT DIVERSIFICATION LOOKS LIKE

Whenever I set up a portfolio with a client, I emphasize the value of discipline and holding steady during periods of volatility. And as I mentioned earlier, I strongly encourage broad diversification. I recommend bonds, stocks, large cap, small cap, and some growth stocks mixed in with value stocks. I advocate for international stocks as well as domestic stocks because more than half the world is in a different market than the United States, and it doesn't make sense to miss those opportunities.

Think of investing the same way you would think about fielding a baseball team. You want to field a full team. You want every position covered. You don't want to have your right fielder wake up one day and say, "I think I'd rather be in left field," and then walk over and stand next to the left fielder. What will you do if the ball is hit to the right? You want your players spread out so you're ready for any play that comes your way.

The same is true for your portfolio. Spread your investments out. Diversify. Cover as many positions as you can. Doing anything other than this conjures up memories of the old Abbott and Costello routine and you may start asking yourself, "Who's on first?"

Maintaining a diversified portfolio also requires patience. Some investors might look at a chart of stock market performance and see that small cap value stocks did better than any other sector over the last ten years. Let's double down on small cap value stocks! When I notice this happening, I pull a Periodic Table of Returns chart. It looks like the periodic table of elements, and it's very revealing. It shows the performance of all the major stock indexes over a multiyear period, and it reveals how an index ranks in returns from one year to the next. No one stays at the top for long, and it's common for an index to record the top returns one year and worst returns the following year. Barclays Aggregate Bond Index, for instance, was one of the few that enjoyed a positive performance in 2008 (5 percent), but the next two years it was at the bottom, even though its returns improved. The Russell 2000 Value Index of small cap value stocks was number one in 2004 and at the bottom by 2007 before shooting back to second place in 2010.

Sound like a roller coaster?

Returns for Asset Classes (1987–2012)

Ranked in Order of Performance (Best to Worst)

Best ← → Worst

Year							
2017	Large Growth	International	Small Growth	S&P 500	Large Value	Small Value	Bonds
2016	Small Value	Large Value	S&P 500	Small Growth	Large Growth	Bonds	International
2015	Large Growth	S&P 500	Bonds	International	Small Growth	Large Value	Small Value
2014	Large Growth	S&P 500	Large Value	Bonds	Small Growth	Small Value	International
2013	Small Growth	Small Value	Large Growth	S&P 500	Large Value	International	Bonds
2012	Small Value	Large Value	International	S&P 500	Large Growth	Small Growth	Bonds
2011	Bonds	Large Growth	S&P 500	Large Value	Small Growth	Small Value	International
2010	Small Growth	Small Value	Large Value	S&P 500	Large Growth	International	Bonds
2009	Small Growth	International	Large Growth	S&P 500	Large Value	Small Value	Bonds
2008	Bonds	Small Value	Large Growth	S&P 500	Small Growth	Large Value	International
2007	International	Large Growth	Small Growth	Bonds	S&P 500	Large Value	Small Value
2006	International	Small Value	Large Value	S&P 500	Small Growth	Large Growth	Bonds
2005	International	Large Value	S&P 500	Small Value	Small Growth	Bonds	Large Growth
2004	Small Value	International	Large Value	Small Growth	S&P 500	Large Growth	Bonds
2003	Small Growth	Small Value	International	Large Value	S&P 500	Large Growth	Bonds
2002	Bonds	Small Value	International	Large Value	S&P 500	Large Growth	Small Growth
2001	Small Value	Bonds	Small Growth	Large Value	S&P 500	Large Growth	International
2000	Small Value	Bonds	Large Value	S&P 500	International	Large Growth	Small Growth
1999	Small Growth	Large Growth	International	S&P 500	Large Value	Bonds	Small Value
1998	Large Growth	S&P 500	International	Large Value	Bonds	Small Growth	Small Value
1997	Large Growth	S&P 500	Small Value	Large Value	Small Growth	Bonds	International
1996	Large Growth	S&P 500	Large Value	Small Value	Small Growth	International	Bonds
1995	Large Growth	S&P 500	Large Value	Small Growth	Small Value	Bonds	International

Going from best to worst is common, but so is going from worst to first. Now, if you had a crystal ball and could predict the future, then you'd know when to move something out of a particular type of stock and put it into another. But no one has a crystal ball. Some people get lucky and make the right call, but more often than not, they give up those great gains in the near future when their "hot hand" at picking investments suddenly turns cold. The best thing you can do is spread your investments out over all these asset classes and build a mix into your portfolio. When one stock rises to the top, you benefit. If it later sinks, it doesn't hurt you because you're catching a ride on another one. This is how you sustain your income over time.

BUILDING YOUR PORTFOLIO

If you are thinking about retiring and have a 401(k) account, you might wonder if you should close that account and reinvest in other stocks and bonds to generate your retirement paycheck.

The answer to that question depends on what funds your 401(k) account includes. Your 401(k) plan may offer a handful of mutual funds, but there are 5,000 mutual funds out there, so if you were my client, I may recommend investing in a mutual fund that's not in your 401(k) lineup.

The same might be true for large cap value stocks. Your 401(k) may offer you only one large cap value fund to choose from. Is that the best large cap value fund out there? Maybe, maybe not. If it's not the best, I would recommend you transfer those funds elsewhere.

Most 401(k) plans have limited options. Account administrators sometimes add funds, but that often means they are chasing a winner, which we know is not a good idea. If you have a 401(k) plan, just think about the number of investment options that have changed over the years. If it is a couple per year and you have only about fifteen funds to choose from, the trustees of your retirement plan are probably chasing recent performance.

Your 401(k) account may include great investments, but it's likely there are better opportunities outside your plan. When that's the case, I'll work with a client to transfer their money out of the 401(k) plan and into an IRA where they are not limited to fund choices inside their plan and have many more (and better) choices of investments. If you don't understand the tax ramifications of removing money from your 401(k) and transferring it into an IRA, then you should talk with a knowledgeable financial advisor or tax advisor.

I often meet people who think their existing portfolio is adequately diversified because they have stock in ten different mutual funds. The problem is that some of those ten funds may be holding the same underlying securities. That would be a problem. I analyze those funds to see where each is invested and how much it overlaps with another fund. If all your investments are in large cap growth stocks, you're not truly diversified. Remember the baseball analogy above? All your players are hanging out in left field.

Up until this point, I have highlighted 401(k)s and mentioned IRAs. They are tax-deferred investment vehicles, which means that any purchase or sales activity that occurs in the account does not create tax liability at the end of the year. In other words, in those tax-deferred accounts, you can have a stock or bond that gains value and then sell it, and there are no tax consequences. You are also not taxed on any dividend or capital gains distributions.

However, outside of IRA, 401(k), and other retirement accounts, a significant factor to consider is how much tax you might owe if you sell one stock to buy another. In a taxable brokerage account, if the original stock cost ten dollars a share, and now it's worth a hundred dollars a share, you must pay taxes on that ninety dollars of gain. However, paying that tax might be worth it if you need to diversify your portfolio.

I've had many clients who own company stock outside

their retirement plans tell me they don't want to sell their stocks and diversify because of the taxes they will pay on the capital gains. Then they watch the value of those shares fall by far more than they would have paid in capital gains. The stock market has a way of charging hefty tuition bills for investors who become too greedy. Bottom line: even if you are facing some hefty tax obligations, I say don't let the tax tail wag the dog.

PLANNING AHEAD

After I've analyzed a client's current portfolio and we have identified any imbalances, limitations, or potential problems, we'll return to the goals and objectives we identified previously for their ideal retirement. How much will they need their portfolio to produce to meet those objectives? This gives us a number to shoot for, and if it is reasonable, we'll then proceed to build a portfolio designed to deliver those types of returns.

There are no guarantees, of course—no one can predict what the stock market will do—but we have the ability to build a diversified portfolio that can absorb many heavy blows. You will be invested in thousands of companies across the globe. If one of those companies suddenly goes bankrupt, you're not even going to notice because you are so globally diversified. It won't be like those who invested their life savings in WorldCom and lost it all when it was revealed the telecommunications giant had cooked its books to hide its losses.

We will build your portfolio with balance and diversity—a mix of stocks, bonds, and cash. Then we pick out how much we want in value versus growth, small cap versus large cap, international versus domestic, and so on. By the time we get down to choosing between mutual fund A or exchange-traded fund product B, each decision is less impactful than the more significant portfolio decisions regarding the breakdown between stocks, bonds, and cash.

It is important to note that when I refer to cash in a retirement account, I'm not talking about your four-to-six-month emergency fund. The cash I'm referring to is essentially your spending money for the next year or two. It's the money you need to have on hand. Whatever you invest in the stock market should be money you aren't going to need for at least five years.

For example, if someone wants to set up a portfolio with me and says they plan to buy a second home in three or four years, I say, "That's great. Let's set that aside and not invest it in the stock market." Some people are surprised by that, so I explain: I have no idea what the stock market is going to do in the next three to five years. We could invest your house money today and find ourselves in a bear market in three years. Your $100,000 could be down to $80,000, and we'll need to keep that money in the market so we can ride it back up and recoup. If you are willing to delay buying that second home for a few years, and we know that initially, then we could invest in stocks. But if you definitely want that second home and the time frame is unquestionably within the next few years, by all means keep the money out of the stock market.

HOW MUCH RISK CAN YOU STOMACH?

These overarching decisions about how much to put in stocks, bonds, and cash are based on each individual's risk tolerance. Each person is different, and often their risk tolerance is influenced by the most recent market returns. So when the market has been going up for a while, most investors take on more risk than they should. The opposite is true when the market has been falling. Investors are scared and often don't have enough stocks in the portfolio to outpace inflation over the long term.

Conservative investors might have 80 percent of their portfolio in bonds and 20 percent in stocks. An aggressive investor would have 20 percent in bonds and 80 percent in stocks. The typical, or what many financial planners call "normal," portfolio is a split of about 60 percent stocks and 40 percent bonds.

At this point, I'll reference a chart I have that shows how these different percentages performed over the last forty years. Here's what that chart looks like.

Sample Historical Volatility
Monthly: 01/1979 – 07/2017

	Fixed	Conservative	Moderate	Normal	Aggressive	Equity
Equity %	0	20	40	60	80	100
Bonds %	100	80	60	40	20	0
Annualized Return	7.59%	8.58%	9.48%	10.29%	11.01%	11.63%
Standard Deviation	5.47	5.72	7.27	9.51	12.05	14.75
Lowest 1-year	−9.20%	−8.96%	−19.04%	−28.22%	−36.57%	−44.14%
Lowest 3-year	1.44%	0.79%	−3.33%	−7.41%	−11.44%	−15.71%
Lowest 5-year	2.02%	2.11%	0.17%	−1.83%	−3.89%	−6.00%
Best 1-year	35.19%	36.14%	42.21%	48.46%	54.88%	61.47%
Best 3-year	19.79%	21.09%	24.03%	27.88%	31.80%	35.74%
Best 5-year	20.29%	20.72%	22.04%	24.85%	27.85%	30.85%

* Equity Portion consists of 70% S&P 500, 15% Russell 2000, and 15% MSCI EAFE. Bonds are 100% Bloomberg Barclays US Aggregate.
** The table is not intended to reflect the actual performance of your investment portfolio.
***Past performance does not guarantee future results.

Across the top, you can see the breakdown of each sample portfolio, with the portfolio on the far left being 100 percent bonds and the portfolio on the far right being 100 percent stocks. Keep in mind that the far right portfolio of 100 percent equities is also a diversified portfolio; it's not stock in one company but in many companies, including large cap and small cap, growth and value, international and domestic.

The second line is the annualized return. As you can see, the return climbs as you go from the most conservative investment (100 percent bonds) to the most aggressive (100 percent stocks). In this sample portfolio using indexes, from 1979 to 2017, the annualized returns ranged from 7.59 percent to 11.63 percent.

If I were to show only these first two lines to clients, most would quickly reach the conclusion that they want to be all in on stocks!

However, as you work your way down the chart, you get a more detailed picture of what those increased returns actually look like over time. When you look at the lowest one-year return, the lowest three-year return, and the lowest five-year return, you start seeing an increasing number of negative numbers. Oh boy. Reality begins to sink in at this point.

If I were all-in on stocks during this period, there was at least one year in which I lost nearly 45 percent of my portfolio's value. One year! And then there was that five-year period where I would have lost 6 percent. That's an average of a 6 percent loss per year for five years in a row. If I were the financial planner who put you in 100 percent stocks and you were a client who called his or her planner every month your portfolio went down, you and I would have been on the phone a lot over that time!

If you're the type of person who can stomach that kind of

situation, then, by all means, invest 100 percent in stocks. As the chart shows, more often than not, you will be compensated for taking on that risk. However, most people don't have that ability. Even though the stock market goes up nearly 75 percent of the time, it is never a steady, long-term climb, and there are often dips and sometimes cliff-like drop-offs. It happens. That's the stock market.

However, if those sharp drops—some of which continue for several months—bother you, put a percentage of your portfolio in bonds. Bonds don't offer a get-rich-quick opportunity, but they are steady, reliable, and modest performers that can continue to make money when equities are tanking. In 2008, for instance, when most stock indexes were losing more than 40 percent of their value, Barclays Aggregate Bond Index was returning 5.24 percent. In 2011, when stocks were flat or losing a little value, Barclays was up nearly 8 percent. When stocks are going gangbusters, as they did in 2009 and 2010, when small cap growth stocks were rebounding with 30 percent returns, bonds can still grow (although Barclays's 6 percent returns those years looked pretty skimpy compared to stock indexes).

Still, this is why you want some bonds in the mix. Bonds, which are more or less an interest-earning loan you are making to a government or some other kind of borrower, moderate what can be a volatile stock market.

Mutual funds help, too. Mutual funds are the cheapest and easiest way to get broad diversification in your stocks. For instance, if you tried to replicate the S&P 500, you would have to split your investment over 500 companies. Even if you had a million dollars to invest, dividing that by 500 companies would give you a pretty small share in many of them. And if you're being charged for buying and selling those tiny shares, the impact of trading fees on your investment fund makes the whole thing cost prohibitive. However, if you overlay that scenario with a mutual fund, such as a Vanguard fund or an S&P index fund, you can buy your shares in one place and gain instant exposure to all 500 companies.

Mutual fund values go up and down, but they also go a long way toward reducing your exposure to many risk factors, such as individual company risk.

For example, say you invested in a restaurant. For a while, it might be the only restaurant in town, and it does good business. Then another restaurant opens up. You instantly have competition and your restaurant's profits go down. When profits go down, that means the overall value of that business also goes down. It is no different in the stock market. Using a different example, if you'd been invested in many restaurants in many towns around the United States at once—through a restaurant mutual fund—the hit taken by one restaurant can be absorbed by all the others, and your personal losses are cushioned.

THE VIRTUES OF REBALANCING

I also recommend rebalancing your portfolio from time to time. Rebalancing is when you sell some of those winners that are doing great and buy some investment in sectors that are cheaper at the time. That may not make sense to everyone, so let me explain why you'd sell a winner for something lower.

Most portfolios maintain a mix of securities and bonds. If you're an aggressive investor, your portfolio might have 80 percent of its assets in stocks, also called securities, and 20 percent in bonds. If you're conservative, the mix might be 20 percent securities and 80 percent bonds. As I mentioned earlier, an average ratio is around 60 percent stocks and 40 percent bonds.

Rebalancing your stocks, funds, or other securities is a way to ensure you keep the right ratio. It also helps you manage how much risk you're willing to live with.

Say you like to keep your portfolio at that sixty-to-forty ratio of stocks to bonds. But then the stock market surges and the value of your stocks climb to become 70 percent of your overall portfolio. Now you've got a higher percentage of your investments tied to the volatility of the stock market and a lower percentage in the less volatile march of the bond market. What do you do?

Rebalance.

That's right, you have to take money from the area that has done very well for you and put it into a stock sector that hasn't been on fire lately but has excellent potential and could do well in the future. It's tempting to put more money into that winner of yours, but that is like driving down the road and looking only at your rearview mirror. Remember, we're hardwired to make the wrong choice in a situation like this, so you have to fight your urge. So rather than trying to ride higher in what might be an overheated balloon, come back down to earth and invest in something that is selling at cheap prices relative to other areas of the stock market. As Warren Buffett likes to say, "Whether buying stocks or socks, I like buying quality merchandise when it is marked down." Rebalancing your portfolio across time is a systematic way of accomplishing this.

Here's an example of what I'm talking about: say you have 60 percent of your portfolio in stocks, 15 percent of which is in small cap stocks. These stocks do so well that in a short time you almost double your $15,000 small cap investment. You're thrilled because of this great return, but now your small cap investment represents a much larger portion of your stock portfolio—much larger than the original plan. Will the growth continue? Maybe, maybe not. Think back to the Periodic Table of Returns we went over, and recall how the Russell 2000 Index of small cap value stocks went from being top dog in 2004 to middle of the pack in 2005 and dead last in 2007. There is no telling when the small cap run will peter out, only that it will end at some point. So you should do the right thing; you should sell some of your high-priced, small cap investments and buy some less expensive stocks and bonds to get your portfolio ratio back to the sixty-to-forty level you established as your portfolio's original allocation.

Remember those investors who bailed out of the stock market during its low period of 2009? Around that time, I recommended that clients rebalance their portfolios. Since stocks had done so poorly, it meant that we were going to sell bonds and buy more stocks. This definitely did not "feel" like the right thing to do. We were all watching the market take drastic falls for more than a year. It felt like every night newscasters were telling us about how badly the market performed that day and there was no end in sight. However, looking back on it now, acting on this simple strategy of rebalancing turned out to be the right move for investors, and they were compensated for doing so over the next few years. Buy low, sell high sounds simple but can be difficult to follow in practice. Rebalancing imposes a discipline to help you do just that.

REDUCING FEES AND TAX OBLIGATIONS

Throughout this process of restructuring a person's portfolio, I'm also looking for ways to keep fees as low as possible—not my fees, which are set and based on a small percentage of your portfolio, but the fees charged by the custodian (e.g., Schwab, TD Ameritrade, or Fidelity) that holds the investment accounts for clients I work with.

For example, if someone were to walk in off the street and open an account with Charles Schwab, they would pay Schwab's retail account fees. A financial planner, on the other hand, has the opportunity to obtain a lower institutional fee from Schwab because Schwab will have to work with only one person—me—and not all the clients I represent.

Another way to reduce fees is to use what are called institutional mutual funds or "institutional pooled accounts." These result when "institutions" arrange "wholesale" funds for the benefit of large investors.

Wealthy individuals and large institutions often use these funds because the minimum investment amounts are usually much higher than what most individuals have

to invest. About 80 percent of all retirement plan investments are in institutional funds, while the vast majority of
individual investors utilize "retail" investment products,
which often come at a higher cost to the investor.

Institutional costs are low because there are no additional
distribution fees; fund companies don't have a lot of small
accounts that need to receive all required documents, dis-
closures, and other administrative requirements. And just
like the Schwab example above, these investment companies know they won't have to staff a large call center
to handle each person's needs because an advisor will be
interacting with most of the individual clients.

The minimum investment required to invest in institutional funds is more than most people can afford.
However, many financial planners have developed
relationships with some of the premier institutional
investment companies, and that relationship gives the
planner's clients access to these investment products.
Working with a financial planner that has access to institutional investment vehicles levels the playing field and
allows the financial planner's clients to enjoy the same
access and benefits that were once only available to much
larger investors.

You can also minimize your investment-related taxes by
using a low-turnover approach to investment decisions.

Whenever there is high turnover in a fund—which is typical for an active manager who is selling Cisco today and buying Microsoft, and then next week is selling the Microsoft and buying Cisco again—realized gains in the mutual fund and the tax liability for those gains are passed on to you, the investor. As a result, high-turnover-type investment vehicles usually have more substantial capital gains tax exposure at the end of the year and that increases your tax bill. Instead, I prefer low-turnover-type investments because they can save on taxes over the years.

This more passive investment approach is becoming increasingly popular. Warren Buffett endorses it. An excellent example of a passive investment is a mutual fund, index fund, or an exchange-traded fund that owns a piece of every company in the S&P 500. Investors do only as good (or as poorly) as all the companies in the S&P 500, which equates to the overall stock market in the United States. What's more, the ongoing annual costs for passive investments like these (called its annual internal-expense ratio) can be much lower than actively managed investments. For example, each year a typical actively managed stock fund might charge $1.25 for every $100 invested, while an index fund would charge only $0.05. Yes, you are seeing that correctly: only five cents! You can see how that would save a lot of money over time with large accounts.

There are plenty of unknowns with investing, but some things we know with certainty. Other factors held constant, reducing an investor's expenses by 1 percent will increase the investment performance by 1 percent. Searching out the lowest-cost exposure to the stock market can directly translate into better investment performance.

We'll talk more about taxes in the next chapter, but let me say here that when it comes to investing, tax obligations can affect how you go about unwinding your 401(k) before and after retirement.

Specifically, at the age of seventy and a half, you are required to start taking distributions and paying tax on those distributions. Some clients I work with choose to begin taking distributions sooner—in their sixties—so that taxes on those distributions are spread out over an extra ten years, or they may be in a lower tax bracket than what we expect in the future. This way, by the time they reach seventy, it's not a huge distribution that increases their tax bill by pushing them into a higher tax bracket. Of course, this doesn't apply to a Roth IRA because you paid taxes on those contributions when you made them. That's one of the most significant advantages of having a Roth IRA over a traditional IRA.

THE IMPACT OF INFLATION

Let's go back to the chart we used earlier in this chapter in the section titled "How Much Risk Can You Stomach?" I want to use it again to talk about a couple of other market forces that affect how we structure your portfolio.

Sample Historical Volatility
Monthly: 01/1979 – 07/2017

	Fixed	Conservative	Moderate	Normal	Aggressive	Equity
Equity %	0	20	40	60	80	100
Bonds %	100	80	60	40	20	0
Annualized Return	7.59%	8.58%	9.48%	10.29%	11.01%	11.63%
Standard Deviation	5.47	5.72	7.27	9.51	12.05	14.75
Lowest 1-year	−9.20%	−8.96%	−19.04%	−28.22%	−36.57%	−44.14%
Lowest 3-year	1.44%	0.79%	−3.33%	−7.41%	−11.44%	−15.71%
Lowest 5-year	2.02%	2.11%	0.17%	−1.83%	−3.89%	−6.00%
Best 1-year	35.19%	36.14%	42.21%	48.46%	54.88%	61.47%
Best 3-year	19.79%	21.09%	24.03%	27.88%	31.80%	35.74%
Best 5-year	20.29%	20.72%	22.04%	24.85%	27.85%	30.85%

* Equity Portion consists of 70% S&P 500, 15% Russell 2000, and 15% MSCI EAFE. Bonds are 100% Bloomberg Barclays US Aggregate.

** The table is not intended to reflect the actual performance of your investment portfolio.

***Past performance does not guarantee future results.

The numbers in our chart showing the returns from bonds versus the returns from stocks might be a little deceptive if you don't take into account inflation. Bonds can help balance out the volatility of stocks, but when you factor in the creeping and invisible specter of inflation, you can quickly see the need for investing in the higher return you get from stocks. The level of inflation varies from year to year, but over time and on average, inflation erodes a little more than 3 percent of your purchasing power each year. Over the course of ten years, a 3 percent inflation rate would turn the purchasing power of a dollar into seventy-four cents.

If you merely converted all your investments to certificates of deposits or some other reliable but low-returning bond, you would not earn enough to keep up with inflation over a thirty-year retirement time frame. As a result, that slow, inexorable march of inflation will require you to eat into your principal very quickly. You need the higher returns and compounding power from stocks to compensate for that inflationary creep and preserve your purchasing power throughout retirement. That said, bonds are nevertheless a life preserver when the stock market starts roiling.

As any investor knows (and as we've noted a few times already), the stock market is volatile. No one can predict just how volatile the market will be, but you can safely predict that there will be volatility. So it is wise to keep things in perspective. Here is a brief overview of actions the market does on a fairly regular basis:

- On average, the stock market has a 14 percent decline at least once a year.
- Daily drops of 2 percent are likely to happen about five times a year.
- A "correction" is signaled by a pullback of more than

10 percent, and a bear market is defined as a pullback of more than 20 percent.

- Bear markets happen about once every five years and their average decline is more than 30 percent. So whenever you hear that the stock market just entered bear market territory, odds are that the declines will continue.

In a bear market, which gets its name from the way a bear swipes downward at its prey, unemployment rises and the economy, in general, slows down. Investors flock to fixed-income securities, and if they want to stay in stocks, they tend to shift their portfolios into consumer staple stocks such as utilities. They do this because people still need water, electricity, and heat regardless of how bad the economy is.

I like to say that bear markets are as common as dirt, which is why you need to build your portfolio with the understanding that stock market drops of 30 percent or more are inevitable.

Even with all this negative information, the important point to remember is that the markets rise almost 75 percent of the time. And over long periods, the stock market does significantly better than inflation, which as we have described, is the real worry during someone's thirty-year retirement.

If you tune in to CNBC and read the newspapers during the next bear market, you'll probably hear that this particular market decline is different from declines in the past. It's the worst anyone has seen, and there is no end in sight. Sometimes, commentators don't even wait for a bear market to start before they start preaching doom and gloom. In fact, as I write this, American businessman Jim Rogers is on television telling his audience that the next bear market will be the worst in his lifetime. He's encouraging investments in all the downtrodden areas of the world economy—sugar, Venezuela, agriculture, and, of course, gold.

However, the next bear market shouldn't be a surprise. It's inevitable. Our last bear market in 2008 brought a 50 percent drop in the stock market, so who knows what the next one will bring? But we do know that one will happen.

Just because bear markets are inevitable doesn't mean they are easy to endure. Bear markets are nerve-wracking, particularly if you are retired and living off your portfolio. But if you've built your portfolio with the right investments and the right mix of stocks, bonds, and cash, you will weather the storm. Knowing what you will do and being prepared for how to react when the next one occurs is the most important concept to think about when things are calm.

COMMON MISTAKES TO AVOID WHEN INVESTING

Investing in the stock market is not always easy. Here are some common mistakes investors make when they invest their money:

- Analysis paralysis, or doing nothing. They take so much time researching and analyzing stocks or mutual funds that they can never find the 100 percent solution to their needs. Here is a point to remember: there are no 100 percent solutions! You need to balance risks with expected returns and then develop a portfolio around those ideas with the best investment you can find at the time. You can only make an educated guess as to what their future returns will be.
- Postponing the start of the race. Regardless of whether you pick the best investment, it's better to start saving and investing as soon as you can. It's like running a marathon around a track. Even if you are slower than the quickest runners, you will still be better off jogging around the track rather than standing at the starting line while others have begun running.
- Being too conservative. Even if you are starting retirement today, you still have thirty-plus years you need to pay for, so don't give up on the stock market. You still need growth to outpace inflation. And if you are younger, you could have fifty or more years to worry about. If that doesn't convince you, just go back and see what the S&P 500 was on the day you were born.

I know I would have loved to be able to put as much money as I could in the market back then.

- Not taking care of high-interest debts. As I mentioned before, large cap US stocks have a historical return of about 10 percent. That won't make up the difference if your credit cards are charging you 16 to 19 percent interest on your balance. Get those paid off as soon as you can.

- Not taking the long view and worrying about what you see or hear on CNBC every night. Invest with the idea that you are not going to look at the investment for another five years. If you need the money sooner, it shouldn't be in the stock market.

- Ignoring ways to get extra free money along the way. Heard of the company match in 401(k) plans? Well, you have to do your part and save money in your 401(k) to receive those free funds. If your employer matches your 401(k) contribution, for example, up to 5 percent of salary, the first 5 percent of your 401(k) contributions have already experienced a 100 percent gain by virtue of your employer's match.

- Viewing collectibles or your house as investments. Don't make the mistake of thinking your jewelry, cars, or your house will be what you use for retirement spending needs. The returns on most real estate and collectibles won't match what the market can do over the long run. Sure, there will be times your house will appreciate, but the long-term averages don't show that it is much more than inflation, especially after you factor in all the needed repairs and upkeep.

- Chasing returns or always trying to have the latest and greatest mutual fund in your portfolio. This is like searching for fool's gold because the investments that have done well in recent years are often not the best going into the future. It's about time in the market, not timing the market.

While the stock market can be confusing to some people, the simple truth is that purchasing equities is an easy way to benefit from the growth of great companies throughout the world. Remember, stocks consistently earn more than other investments, and they give you the opportunity to benefit from the miracle of compound interest. The crucial strategies we've identified here—such as diversifying and rebalancing—will help you on your way.

CHAPTER 6

THE ROLE OF THE GOVERNMENT

Just as I preach patience to my clients who invest in the stock market, I also preach patience when it comes to dealing with the federal government for your Social Security and Medicare benefits.

These are excellent benefits for retirees, but they can be confusing, particularly if you have special circumstances. This chapter will give you an overview and highlight typical circumstances many face, but it's impossible to cover every possible scenario. When planning your retirement, expect to do some research to determine the best options for your personal situation.

What people have a hard time understanding is that even

though you are entitled to Social Security payments—and not everyone is, including many teachers, railroad employees, and people who worked for state governments—your payments at sixty-two will be about 30 percent less than if you wait until full retirement at sixty-six or sixty-seven. If you're sixty-seven and you can hold out until you're seventy, the benefit goes up even more.

Here's a typical scenario for someone born in 1956. Say this person worked all his life and is making just over $100,000 a year at the age of sixty-two. If this person were to start taking benefits right away, he would get about $1,920 a month. If they wait until full retirement (sixty-six years and four months), that monthly payment would go up to $2,665. That's nearly 40 percent more. Now, if they wait until they are seventy years old, the monthly check goes to $3,508. That's a walloping 82 percent higher than if they'd started taking payments at age sixty-two!

That translates into an 8 percent annual return on your Social Security benefit. That's huge. I would love to be able to tell my clients that I can get them a guaranteed 8 percent return on their stock portfolio! The government is giving it to you. You just need to be able to delay taking your benefits.

So, in many situations, I tell people to delay taking Social

Security as long as you can. I know, I know: you could get hit by the bread truck in a couple of years and not get anything out of Social Security. But that's not the point. The point is that if you can wait, wait. If you're working and doing well and you don't need the money, you'll get a much higher paycheck if you hold off on taking the benefit.

MAKING ADJUSTMENTS TO SOCIAL SECURITY

One thing to keep in mind is that Social Security was never meant to be a person's sole source of income in retirement. As President Eisenhower said, "The system is not intended as a substitute for private savings, pension plans, and insurance protection. It is, rather, intended as the foundation upon which these other forms of protection can be soundly built." And according to the Social Security Administration (SSA), benefits are designed to replace only about 40 percent of the average worker's wages in retirement. So while it may be a large part of your retirement income, you should not plan for it to be the *only* source of income.

The benefit you'll receive is based on the thirty-five highest years of your earning history—with adjustments for inflation. The SSA estimates that Social Security payments typically make up about a third of a retiree's annual income.

Another aspect of Social Security that many aren't aware of is this: you can stop taking the benefit within a specific time frame and hit the reset button. Say you began receiving benefits at age sixty-two but have a change of heart and realize you'd rather wait until you're seventy. If your decision comes within the first twelve months of applying for benefits, you can withdraw your claim, pay back the benefits you received, and file again later. You are allowed only one opportunity to withdraw a benefits claim, however.

When you reach full retirement age (which is calculated based on the year you were born), you can ask the SSA to suspend payments until you reach seventy. This is when the guaranteed 8 percent return comes into play. During the time you have suspended your SSA payments (between your full retirement age and the age of seventy), your benefit will increase at an 8 percent annual rate.

BENEFITS FOR MARRIED COUPLES

Another thing people don't realize is how favorable the system is for married couples. A married couple can receive both of their individual Social Security benefits that they've accrued throughout their life, or the non-working spouse can receive a "homemakers" benefit that equates to half of the breadwinner's benefit. So if the wife was the primary breadwinner for the family, the husband's Social Security check could amount to half of the wife's benefits—provided that half of the wife's check is greater than what the husband would receive from his own earnings history. Not a bad deal at all.

If one half of a married couple dies, the survivor won't get both benefit checks but will receive a check equal to the larger of the two. Leaving something for your surviving spouse is another reason for delaying your benefit until the age of seventy—particularly if your spouse is younger than you.

If you're a married couple thinking about retirement and Social Security benefits, it pays to plan a little. If one spouse applies for benefits before full retirement age, his earnings will be permanently reduced by a percentage calculated by the number of months until full retirement. However, a widow's benefit would not be reduced as long as the surviving spouse was beyond their full retirement age (FRA).

To help explain this, let's use an example where the breadwinner is age sixty-six, and the nonworking spouse is sixty-two. They both can apply for benefits at the same time. The breadwinner will receive his or her full benefit (let's say $2,000). The spouse will apply for spousal benefits, which equates to $1,000 in this scenario. However, because the nonworking spouse is only sixty-two, those benefits will be reduced by about 30 percent. So in this scenario, this couple can start collecting $2,700 per month right away.

Now, what happens if the breadwinner passes away? It depends on how old the nonworking spouse is at that time. Some people think that because the nonworking spouse took his or her benefits early, the survivor's benefit would also be reduced. But that is not the case. It depends on how old the nonworking spouse is at the time he or she starts to receive the widow's benefit. If the nonworking spouse is above their FRA, then the benefits are not reduced. If below FRA, the benefits would be reduced based on the nonworking spouse's age at that time and how many months it was before FRA.

When calculating your Social Security benefit, the SSA looks at your highest thirty-five years of income, regardless of when they occur. If you continue working after receiving benefits, the SSA will recalculate your benefit amount and could increase it if you make enough. Your benefit will increase if the income you earn during those additional years is more than what you earned in one of your existing thirty-five years of income. But remember, receiving benefits is based on having ten years' worth of income. If you have only the minimum, that means you'll have twenty-five years of $0 of income in the calculation.

In this case, any additional year you work will definitely help your situation.

However, if you're younger than FRA when you start taking benefits, and you're still working, the SSA will reduce your benefit by $1 for every $2 you earn over the limit. That is a big deduction! For the year 2018, this limit on earned income is $17,040 ($1,420 per month), and it increases slightly every year. It's a penalty the government put in place because they want you to wait until you are at your FRA before collecting benefits.

After FRA, you can earn as much as you want and not lose any benefits. You likely will still have to pay taxes on your Social Security income. However, you only pay taxes on up to 85 percent of your entire benefit if you're filing a joint return and earned more than $44,000. You only pay taxes on 50 percent of your benefit if you make less than $44,000 as a couple or less than $34,000 as an individual. If your benefit is less than $32,000 as a couple (and $25,000 as an individual), you don't pay any taxes. These levels of income that subject your Social Security to income tax change over time. But regardless of the amount, you can get the SSA to withhold a portion of your payment to cover your taxes. It's important to note that many states don't tax Social Security benefits.

Social Security claiming strategies can be very confusing.

That's why even after I talk through the mechanics of how it works, I still recommend clients schedule an appointment with Social Security a year or two before they would like to start taking benefits. The clerk at the office will print your specific earnings history and calculate your exact benefits. They can also answer any additional questions you might have. However, I strongly recommend that clients don't suddenly decide to start taking benefits at that initial meeting. Take some time and think about how some different scenarios impact your decisions.

PLANNING FOR HEALTHCARE

I often have new clients tell me that they would like to retire early. The first question I have for them is, "OK, that sounds good. But what are you planning to do about healthcare?"

It is a critical issue to consider because it is often the area that derails plans to retire early. The current age to qualify for Medicare is sixty-five, so if you are planning to retire before then, you need a plan to cover your healthcare until Medicare kicks in. Most people understand the need to have a certain amount of assets saved, but they fail to understand the implication of leaving the workforce at fifty-five and covering themselves with health insurance for the next ten years. Some people will receive retiree benefits from their former company, but other early retirees are going to have to set aside funds to cover healthcare costs.

And this is no small amount. The average health insurance policy for one person who is fifty-five to sixty-four years old can average more than $8,500 per year. Add a spouse to the plan and those costs double. Furthermore, the average deductible for a family can be more than $8,000 per year. When you add it all up, early retirement doesn't look so good for many people. As a result, many choose to wait a few years to retire, and some will wait until Medicare becomes their health insurance option.

Medicare is a great system for our retirees, but as I mentioned earlier, it can be very confusing. Here is a quick breakdown of what you need to know about it.

Medicare is a federal health insurance program for US citizens and legal permanent residents of more than five continuous years. Most people become eligible for Medicare when they turn sixty-five or are disabled. You may also qualify for Medicare at any age if you have end-stage renal disease requiring dialysis, a kidney transplant, or amyotrophic lateral sclerosis, or ALS, also known as Lou Gehrig's disease.

There are two primary parts of Medicare—Part A, which

covers hospital costs, and Part B, which is for medical coverage.

Medicare Part A coverage includes inpatient hospital, skilled nursing facility, hospice, and eligible home healthcare. The covered hospital services usually include medically required services and equipment to treat your ailment. This can include a semiprivate room, general nursing services, and prescription drugs. Coverage may also provide for certain home health services, including physical therapy, speech-language pathology, occupational therapy, or speech therapy services for a period of time.

Before you turn sixty-five, you should contact the SSA to start your Medicare coverage. Most people are automatically enrolled in the free version of Part A if they worked at least ten years and paid Medicare taxes while working. You can also sign up for it and pay a monthly premium if you haven't worked long enough to earn Part A for free. If your spouse qualifies for Part A without a premium, you'll be eligible to obtain premium-free Part A coverage based on your spouse's years of employment. Having said all of this, your Medicare Part A coverage comes with other costs, including deductibles, coinsurance, and copayments. So it isn't really completely free.

A crucial detail about Part A coverage is that it doesn't

include long-term nursing care. Part A covers only costs associated with a skilled nursing facility care where your personal care needs (e.g., bathing and eating) aren't the only type of care you require.

Medicare Part B coverage includes medically necessary outpatient services, including doctor visits, medical equipment, lab tests, ambulance services, mental healthcare, and other preventive services.

Part B coverage includes a variety of preventive services to keep you healthy. This includes annual physicals, tests for various diseases and health conditions, nutrition therapy, tobacco cessation counseling, and certain vaccines, such as flu shots.

Part B has a very limited prescription drug coverage. Only certain types of medications that are usually administered by a doctor are covered, including injectable drugs or medications given by infusion. For all other prescription drug benefits, you'll need to sign up for Medicare Part D coverage.

Unlike Part A, you will pay a monthly premium for Part B, which varies each year. And just like Part A, other costs related to your Part B coverage may include deductibles, copayments, and coinsurance costs. Because costs can vary by doctor, hospital, or region of the country, you should always check the cost before receiving the service.

Once you're enrolled in Part A and/or Part B, you will have other coverage options to choose from.

Medicare Part C coverage is often known as Medicare Advantage plans. It covers services from a Medicare-approved private insurance company. These plans are required to cover at least the same level of benefits that you'd have under Part A and Part B.

In addition to what's covered under normal Medicare health insurance, some Part C plans offer other benefits, such as routine dental and vision, wellness programs, hearing care, and prescription drug coverage. There are many types of Medicare Advantage plans, such as Preferred Provider Organization (PPO) plans and Health Maintenance Organization (HMO) plans.

It's important to understand that even though you're receiving benefits from a private insurance company, you're still enrolled in Medicare. You've just chosen to obtain coverage from a particular company instead of through the federal health insurance program.

Medicare Part D coverage provides additional drug benefits while you are enrolled in Part A and Part B for your hospital and medical coverage. As mentioned above, Medicare offers limited prescription drug benefits, and you're only covered for medications in certain situations. You can now sign up for Medicare Part D prescription drug coverage through a separate drug plan.

If you take prescription drugs and want additional insurance to cover those costs, make sure the plan you're considering covers your medications. You can check this by looking at the plan's list of covered drugs. Every Medicare drug plan includes a list and it's usually posted online. Keep in mind that the drugs covered can (and often do) change.

Medicare Supplement, or what is known as Medigap coverage, may help pay for out-of-pocket costs not covered in Part A or B, including costs such as copayments, coinsurance, deductibles, and overseas health coverage. Just like the list of covered prescription drugs, you can learn a lot more about this type of coverage by checking out the company's Medicare Supplement services online.

Even after I go through all this information about Medicare and all of its various options, my clients usually ask me, "So what choice should we make regarding our Medicare coverage?" My only answer to this question is, "Well, it depends." It depends on a lot of things. You might start by considering the factors that are important to you. For example, do you travel and don't want to worry about provider options? Under regular Medicare, you can receive services from any doctor who accepts Medicare.

Do you go to the doctor frequently and as a result have high out-of-pocket costs? A Medicare Supplement plan can help cover those costs. You may be interested in coverage beyond Medicare, such as vision or wellness programs. In these situations, Medicare Advantage providers in your area would be an option to consider.

There are many ways to analyze your individual situation. Take your time and do the research. It will help you make an informed decision and will limit the number of times you are surprised by how the programs work for you.

YOUR BIGGEST RETIREMENT EXPENSE: TAXES

Most of us, while we're working, don't pay much attention to taxes. When we get our paychecks, all the taxes have already been deducted, and it was like the money was never ours in the first place.

In retirement, it's different. In retirement, when you are coming up with your own paycheck, it's important to pay close attention to taxes—how you pay them, when, and how much you owe. Taxes can dictate how much you withdraw from your retirement accounts and which accounts you choose to draw from. Retirement paychecks can come from a variety of sources—Social Security, 401(k) accounts, taxable investment accounts, Roth IRAs, and possibly a part-time job—so it's important to stay on top of where that money is coming from so you can be sure to set aside enough for your tax bill.

The first thing to take into consideration is your tax bracket. We all know that the more you make, the more you have to pay in taxes. Your tax bracket—the percentage of your income that goes to the government—increases as your income increases. That is why you should know what your "marginal" income tax rate is. Your marginal rate is simply the rate of taxes you will pay for the next dollar of income you receive. It's a sliding scale and sometimes you want to have enough income to cover your expenses but not so much more that it will cause you to jump to the next higher tax bracket.

In retirement, one goal should be to keep your tax bracket at a level you are comfortable with. For example, the current tax rate for a couple making between $19,000 and $78,000 a year is 12 percent, but for those who earn between $168,000 and $321,000, the tax rate climbs to 24 percent. That's a significant difference, and it could influence when you retire and how you handle your benefits.

Here is another situation to consider. If you're an executive who has stock options, I would recommend that you retire in December but not liquidate your stock options until the following year. If you cashed in that stock in the same year you retired, it could be enough to throw you into that higher income bracket, and you would be required to pay more in taxes. But if you hold off a bit—you usually have to liquidate stock options within ninety days—you throw that additional money into a different year, saving you a hefty tax bill.

Keeping your income and taxes at a predictable and manageable level is another good reason for paying off your big debts—such as your mortgage—before retirement. If you have fewer expenses, you will need less income coming from your retirement assets, and that will also keep your taxes down.

STRATEGIES FOR REDUCING YOUR TAX BILL

We've already discussed how the federal government taxes your Social Security—it taxes up to 85 percent of your benefit and can withhold those taxes for you—but the taxes you pay on your other sources of income depend on what those sources are.

For example, if you take distributions from a Roth IRA after age fifty-nine and a half, you don't pay taxes on the amount because you paid your taxes when you put the money in the account. But if you are withdrawing from a tax-deferred account, such as a 401(k), Uncle Sam will be standing nearby to collect his cut. That is why it's crucial that you avoid withdrawals that will bump you into a higher tax bracket.

Another concern is for retirees who are seventy and older. These folks have to take a required minimum distribution (RMD) from their tax-deferred accounts, including 401(k), 403(b), and regular IRA accounts. These required distributions are noteworthy because if you don't take them, the IRS can assess a penalty equal to 50 percent of the amount you were supposed to withdraw. I don't know how many times I've had to call clients and remind them to take these distributions. In fact, my RMD process has me triple-checking each client's account to make sure we've taken the required distribution amount each year.

IRA DISTRIBUTION STRATEGIES

Normally, IRA RMDs begin when you reach the age of seventy and a half. The distribution requirements dictated by the IRS are strict. This can be an issue for people who are required to distribute a large amount from their IRA each year because all of that money is taxable income.

If you don't need this money, one strategy is called a Qualified Charitable Distribution (QCD.) A QCD allows individuals who are seventy and a half and older to transfer up to $100,000 directly from their IRA to an IRS-approved charity. The most important part is that the transfer can offset the amount of your RMD for the year. The transferred amount is not taxed as income and although it can't be used as a charitable deduction, the entire amount is not included in your income for tax purposes. There are some specific tax requirements that must be met, but overall, if you have charitable intent and more income than you need from your IRA RMDs, a QCD is a great strategy to investigate.

If you still need income after receiving your Social Security and RMD distributions, it might make sense to take money from your taxable accounts, such as your brokerage account. When you do this, you will likely have to sell investments, in which case you'll have to pay capital gains taxes on any appreciation. In these cases, the capital gains taxes are usually less than your marginal income tax rate under current tax law.

For most taxpayers, long-term capital gains (those investments you've held for more than one year) are taxed at a rate of 15 percent or less, and some will qualify for a 0 percent tax rate on long-term capital gains. The highest possible capital gains tax rate is 20 percent, but even that is lower than the highest marginal income tax rate of 37 percent.

One strategy people use to minimize their taxes is to start taking distributions from their tax-deferred accounts years before those RMDs start. You reduce your overall balance so that your RMD—and the taxes you need to pay on it—can be reduced.

Tax strategies are vital when you're talking about taxable accounts, such as your brokerage account or certificates of deposit. Reducing capital gains and dividends will help reduce your tax burden. This might mean that you try to avoid selling securities at a gain and the additional taxes as a result. It might also mean holding on to investments a little longer so that you have owned them for more than a year. When you do that, you pay taxes on long-term capital gains instead of short-term capital gains, which are taxed at a higher rate.

You also have the ability to conduct tax-loss harvesting in your taxable accounts. Tax-loss harvesting is when you use the "tax loss" of one investment to offset the gains you might capture in another investment. Tax-loss harvesting involves the sale of a current position and the purchase of a proxy security for thirty days. You purchase a proxy security (one that is similar but not exactly the same) so that you will still remain invested in order to receive gains if they occur during that time. But you can capture the tax loss and use it to reduce your income taxes. After thirty days, you then sell the proxy investments and repurchase your original holdings. This is done to avoid the thirty-day IRS wash sales rules and to allow you to remain invested throughout the time period.

Tax-loss harvesting is a great way to reduce current and future taxes. If properly applied, it can save you taxes and help you diversify your portfolio in ways you may not have considered. For example, a loss in the value of security A could be sold to offset the increase in value of security B, thus eliminating a capital gains tax liability. Furthermore, tax losses can be used to offset year-end mutual fund capital gain distributions, and individuals can deduct up to $3,000 in capital losses each year against their taxable income. Under current tax law, unused losses can be carried forward indefinitely.

Another avenue some people follow is purchasing municipal bonds. Although most bond interest payments are taxed at your marginal rate, interest on municipal bonds are not taxed by the federal government at all. Depending on where you live, you might also avoid state taxes. There are a couple of drawbacks, however. Tax-free bonds usually pay a lower interest rate than other bonds, and this nontaxable interest influences how much tax you pay on Social Security benefits. You'll have to decide if the tax break is worth the lower return. For most situations, if you are in a high marginal tax bracket, then municipal bonds are a great option to consider for taxable accounts.

THE INS AND OUTS OF RETIREMENT ACCOUNTS

There are many different types of retirement plans and terms used to describe them. For simplicity sake, we can say a retirement plan is typically an employer-provided plan or an Individual Retirement Account (IRA).

EMPLOYER-SPONSORED RETIREMENT PLANS

An employer-sponsored plan is a type of benefit offered to employees of a company or organization. When you enroll in a plan, you often receive tax advantages and matching benefits that your employer may be required to provide to participants. Employer contributions may require that you stay with the company for a certain time, which is called the vesting schedule. Regardless of the vesting schedule, if you are not contributing up to the company match, you may be ignoring a significant employee benefit.

Employee retirement plans are a systematic way of saving for your retirement. Employers provide these plans for the tax breaks they get from the IRS, but also because the plans allow employers to hire and retain valuable employees. There are many specifications to these plans that an employer needs to consider, but employees have little control over adjusting plan options.

401(k) plans

Contributions to a 401(k) plan are made using pretax dollars. Pretax means money is taken from your paycheck and put into your account before taxes are taken. Consequently, your income taxes are lowered. If you earn $50,000 and contribute $5,000, you are taxed only on $45,000 of income.

Additionally, 401(k) investment gains grow tax deferred until you withdraw the funds, usually during retirement. If you withdraw funds from the plan before retirement age, you could pay a 10 percent penalty on top of federal, state, and local income taxes. Some employers allow you to take loans from your 401(k), but I rarely recommend that because of problems caused if you lose your job or leave the company.

Some variations of the 401(k) plans are 403(b) and 457(b) plans. A 403(b) is typically offered to educators and nonprofit workers. A 457(b) plan is typically available to government employees.

Roth 401(k)

A Roth 401(k) is like a regular 401(k), but you contribute money to the plan on an after-tax basis. The Roth contribution goes from your paycheck into your account after income taxes have been taken out. The trade-off is that qualified withdrawals are *tax free* versus fully taxable at your marginal rate the way 401(k) distributions are. A Roth 401(k) plan is a particularly useful tool if you end up in a higher tax bracket upon retirement. I usually recommend young workers who are just starting their careers and don't have a high income yet to seriously consider a Roth 401(k) if it is available to them.

SIMPLE IRA

The Savings Incentive Match for Employees IRA (SIMPLE IRA) is a retirement plan small companies can offer employees. A SIMPLE IRA works like a 401(k); contributions are made from pretax paycheck withdrawals, and the money grows tax deferred until retirement.

SEP IRA

A Simplified Employee Pension (SEP) IRA allows self-employed individuals to contribute a portion of their income to a retirement account and fully deduct the contributions from income taxes. It works much like a regular 401(k).

For all of these employee-sponsored plans, once you reach the age of fifty, the government allows you to make what's called catch-up contributions. Congress added the new catch-up option to encourage older workers to save more for retirement. All it means is that after you contribute the maximum regular contribution, you can make additional catch-up contributions. Catch-up contributions are possible in 401(k), 403(b), and 457 plans. You can only make catch-up contributions if your plan allows them, but 90 percent of them do.

IRAS

An IRA is an individual account set up at a financial institution that allows you to save for retirement on a tax-deferred or tax-free basis depending on the type of IRA you establish. There are two main types of IRAs—traditional and Roth—and each comes with different tax ramifications.

However, all IRAs are set up so you can't access the funds until you are fifty-nine-and-a-half without incurring a 10 percent penalty. While there are some situations where you can access the funds without paying a penalty (paying college expenses, paying medical expenses greater than 10 percent of your adjusted gross income, paying for a first-time home purchase up to $10,000, and paying for the costs of a sudden disability), I tell my clients that these accounts are for retirement and should be invested for the long term.

With a **traditional IRA**, you make contributions with

money that you may be able to deduct on your tax return, and any earnings can potentially grow tax deferred until you withdraw them in retirement. Many retirees also find themselves in a lower tax bracket when they retire compared to the several years prior to retirement, so the tax-deferral means the money may be taxed at a lower rate.

With a **Roth IRA**, you contribute money you've already paid taxes on. Your money then grows tax-free, with tax-free withdrawals in retirement as long as you follow the guidelines. In the same example we used earlier in the chapter, you would pay income tax on your full earnings ($50,000) and then put the $5,000 savings into the account. When you retire, you can withdraw that $5,000 without having to pay tax on it.

It also grows tax-free each year so you won't pay taxes on dividends and capital gains like you do in a normal taxable investment account. There are income limitations for being able to contribute to a Roth IRA, however, and if you are above that, the only way to contribute is through a backdoor Roth IRA contribution. These are tricky and the rules are strict, so if you're going to do this, consult a financial or tax advisor. It's a complicated, multistep process, and if you do any of the steps incorrectly, the tax ramifications can be massive.

A **Rollover IRA** is nothing more than a traditional IRA

that has money that was "rolled over" from another qualified retirement plan, such as a 401(k) or 403(b). I don't think of it as a separate type of account. Several years ago, it was important to keep that money separated because old tax laws only allowed you to transfer rollover IRAs back into another employer-sponsored plan. That requirement has since been eliminated, but you still see some accounts titled *rollover* and *traditional*.

As with employer-sponsored plans, individual retirement accounts also allow catch-up contributions for people over the age of fifty.

A **Stretch IRA** is not a formal account or a type of investment but a simple strategy that enables you to extend the tax-deferred growth of an inherited IRA. You are still required to take distributions, but there are several strategies for maximizing the value of your inheritance, giving the IRA more time to capitalize on compound interest.

Regardless of the type of IRA you inherit, if you are a non-spouse beneficiary, you must take RMDs based on the IRS's life expectancy table. The younger the beneficiary, the lower the RMD. This allows more funds to remain in the IRA account, and it allows the distribution to stretch out over a long time. Some people incorporate this into their planning strategy by passing on IRA assets to younger members of the family. If there are enough assets to take care of a surviving spouse that are outside the IRA, naming a child or grandchild is a great way to transfer wealth across generations.

Most IRA owners name their spouse as the primary beneficiary and their children as the contingent beneficiaries. While there is nothing wrong with this approach, it could force the spouse to take more distributions (taxable income!) from the account compared to what he or she really needs. If income needs are not an issue for the spouse, then naming younger beneficiaries can make sense. The key with utilizing the stretch IRA strategy is that the beneficiary needs to take distributions fairly soon after someone dies. So working with your accountant or financial planner becomes critical at this time.

CHOOSING THE RIGHT ACCOUNT

One of the critical retirement decisions that you make during your working career is deciding what kind of retirement account you want to put your savings into. Most people opt for a traditional IRA account, or if it's through their employer, a 401(k) account. These accounts allow you to save money, reduce your current taxes, and let your money grow tax deferred, which means you don't pay income taxes until you take distributions during retirement.

If you're just starting out in your career, you have to

decide which type of account is best for you—a pretax account such as an IRA or 401(k) or an after-tax account such as a Roth IRA or Roth 401(k).

For most people, the underlying consideration is this: will your tax rate in retirement be higher than it is now? For many young people, the answer is that their tax rate is likely to be higher later in life when they reach their peak earning potential. For them, a Roth IRA makes a lot of sense. If they are still keen on getting that tax deduction from their traditional 401(k), I'll recommend that they put a little bit in both kinds of accounts. A 401(k) and a Roth IRA are a great combination. As we've already seen, it's nice to have a Roth account you can draw from in retirement because you don't run as much of a risk of bumping up your income and landing in a higher tax bracket.

IRAs are tricky for high-wage earners. Although the Economic Recovery Tax Act of 1981 made tax-deferred IRA contributions available to anyone with an earned income, the law was changed in 1986 and placed limits on those contributions for high-income workers who were also covered by a plan through their employer. If you have a 401(k) through work, for instance, you are still allowed to make tax-deductible contributions to an IRA in addition to the amount you put into your 401(k) account but only up to a certain point. The income limit changes from year to year. If your income is above the IRA contribution limit, you can still contribute to an IRA, but you can't deduct those contributions on your tax return. With income above the IRA contribution limit, you lose your deduction for a contribution to an IRA, but you will still be able to benefit from tax-deferred growth on the money.

The limit led to some people mingling after-tax IRA contributions with pretax contributions, which, as you can imagine, can get pretty messy. You've already paid income taxes on some of your IRA money but must still pay taxes on the remainder when you pull it out. People in this position have to file forms with the IRS so the government can prorate your distributions to account for the taxes they've already paid on those payments. If you don't do it correctly, you wind up paying taxes twice on some of your retirement savings!

When I have clients who are in this position, I recommend that instead of putting after-tax contributions into their IRA, they just put their money into a regular taxable account. You don't have to wait until you're fifty-nine and a half to withdraw the money. You also can put the money into tax-efficient investments with low turnover inside of it. This is important because it means you're not hit with a whole host of capital gains and dividend distributions that you will be taxed on throughout the years of growth in the account. Yes, you will still have some taxes to pay, but having the freedom to use the funds anytime you want, and for whatever you want, is a nice benefit for investing this way.

Taxes, as you can see, get a little more complicated after retirement. It's a balancing act where you have to determine whether the amount you earn on an investment is worth the amount you lose to taxes. This is why a lot of people enlist the help of a financial planner.

GETTING THOSE TAXES PAID

Figuring out your tax bill in retirement is one challenge. Figuring out how to pay those taxes is another.

While many workers in the United States have their taxes deducted automatically, many retirees have to set up a payment system to ensure they pay taxes throughout the year. The IRS doesn't like to wait around all year for you to pay your taxes. You can't wait until December and write one big check. If you do, the IRS will penalize you.

Consequently, many people estimate what their annual taxes will be and then send the IRS quarterly installments on that bill. Those are due in April, June, September, and January. Small business owners are used to making quarterly estimated tax payments, but for most people, it's a new thing.

You can also set it up so that your custodian (e.g., Schwab, Fidelity, TD Ameritrade, etc.) that holds your IRA account withholds taxes to pay the federal government a percentage of each distribution from your tax-deferred investment account. And, as we mentioned earlier, the SSA will automatically withhold taxes from your regular benefit check. You can choose to have 7 percent, 10 percent, 15 percent, or 25 percent withheld. You just have to file Form W-4V with the SSA to make that happen.

Although the IRS frowns on large, end-of-the-year tax payments instead of quarterly payments, you can wait until the end of the year to pay if you use withholding. One strategy is to wait until December to take your RMD and use that required minimum distribution as your tax payment.

You have many choices in how you decide to take care of your taxes, but it is important to have a plan.

THE SCOOP ON ANNUITIES

Many retirees are attracted to annuities, which involve paying an insurance company a lump sum in return for regular monthly payments for the rest of your life. The insurance company invests your money, but you don't share in the profits, although some index annuities allow investors to enjoy some limited growth—something on the order of 4 percent per year.

Some people like annuities because it insulates them from the vagaries of the stock market. These investors have heard horror stories about retirees losing all their money in the stock market and having to take jobs driving a school bus or something. With an annuity, you don't have to worry about how your lump sum payment to the insurance company is doing in the stock market; you just get your monthly check, no matter how bad it gets. And, if you live a long time, you can actually get a good return on your initial annuity investment; you're betting the insurance company that you will live longer than they think you will. But quite often, you need to live significantly longer than average mortality rates to recoup your investment.

On the other hand, if you get hit by that proverbial bread truck two years after buying an annuity, you lose (in more ways than one) and the insurance company wins. Some annuities allow payments to heirs to continue for a set time, but those options cost extra.

Generally speaking, I don't like annuities for my clients. In some cases, they might make sense, but in most instances, people can do better investing in a diversified portfolio of stocks and bonds. There are ways to protect your money when the market is going through gyrations. Annuities play on people's uncertainty about the stock market, but the reality is that the market, while volatile, dependably comes back. The bottom line is that you are paying a price to the insurance company to receive a feeling of security.

The other thing people must realize about annuities is their cost. The commissions and fees are usually very high, although some companies such as Vanguard offer lower-cost accounts. Still, I like to say annuities are not bought; they're sold. Most people don't walk into an investment broker's office or a financial advisor's office and say, "I want to buy an annuity!" But some walk out with an annuity because a salesperson managed to convince them that the stock market could possibly wipe them out. The bottom line is that annuities are an insurance product sold by insurance salespeople with an inherent conflict of interest. Their compensation is directly correlated to how many annuity contracts they can sell. Fortunately, I don't work that way with my clients.

MAKING SENSE OF IT ALL

Most of us think of retirement as a relaxed time—a time in our life when we can stop worrying about income taxes and issues related to them. And it should be that way. However, retirement requires that you pay close attention to not only your government benefits, such as your Social Security check, but also your government obligations—your tax bill. A big driver in your tax bill will be your tax bracket and how you handle your investments to minimize the impact of taxes on your nest egg.

A little bit of strategy can go a long way toward helping you, particularly if you have several accounts. After your RMDs, what accounts should you draw from first—your taxable accounts or your tax-deferred accounts? Are you paying taxes twice on some of that money? If you're selling investments, should you sell the winners or the losers?

A trusted advisor can help you sort through those issues and help you make the right choices. Keep that in mind as we move on to the next chapter and figure out where your new paycheck will come from.

CHAPTER 7

MAKING YOUR NEW PAYCHECK

Most of us who have held jobs with companies or governments have never really thought much about where our paycheck comes from or how the payroll department generated our checks each month. Somebody just came around and handed us the envelope, or we logged into our bank accounts and saw our weekly or monthly salary neatly recorded. I wouldn't say we all took that check for granted, but we did expect it would be there at the end of the week, or every two weeks, or what's more common today, every month. Occasionally, if you have auto deposit, you might log in to your employee dashboard and take a look at your monthly pay stub to see how much you are contributing to your 401(k) and how much your employer is matching that contribution.

When you retire, that paycheck goes away, and it becomes your responsibility to figure out where your monthly salary will come from. How much will you get from Social Security? How much will you take from your investments? How do you get your money transferred into your checking account so you have the cash to buy coffee, or pay your bills, or take that quick trip to Colorado to visit your grandkids? These are all real-life questions that come with retirement, so let's talk a bit about what your options are.

One of the first steps in setting up your retirement paycheck is scheduling appointments with the human resources department of your employer and with the SSA. Your HR department will help you navigate through the retirement process and explain to you any lingering issues related to your employment. Will you continue with the company in a part-time capacity? If you're younger than sixty-five, will the company keep you on its health insurance policy until you qualify for Medicare? If your company or government agency is one of the few who still offer pensions, HR will walk you through the process of determining your pension payments, which could be based on the number of years you have with the company and how much you've earned in salary. Your salary at retirement will be particularly important when you calculate these benefits.

Likewise, the SSA will walk you through the process for

signing up for your Social Security benefits and figuring out what taxes to deduct and what accounts you want your funds deposited in. The quickest and easiest way to sign up for retirement benefits is online, but you can also do it over the phone or in person at your local SSA office. As we discussed earlier, you most likely will have already had an appointment with the SSA in the years leading up to retirement, so filing for benefits will be very easy. I tell my clients to schedule a later afternoon appointment at the SSA and then take yourselves out for a nice dinner to celebrate afterward.

USING YOUR INVESTMENTS

Once all those items are checked off your to-do list, the next step is to look at your investments and figure out how to use them to build the rest of your retirement paycheck.

There are three schools of thought on how to do this, but the approach is similar for each.

The first approach uses reverse dollar cost averaging, where you have one investment that you're using as your distribution fund. This fund usually is a balanced mutual fund that has a set amount of stocks, bonds, large cap, small cap, value, growth, and international stocks all encompassed in that one fund. You merely put this account on autopilot and take a distribution of, say,

$2,000, from it every month. You are not forced to make a decision on what to sell because it's a single fund and it's already balanced, so the money might be coming from a wide variety of different stocks held by the mutual fund. When you are buying shares on a regular basis, it's called dollar cost averaging. When you are withdrawing in the same fashion as we just described, it's called reverse dollar cost averaging.

Early in the process, the value of your investments should still be growing larger each year, but later in your retirement, you may start eating into the principal. That moment is called the inflection point. At that juncture, your overall wealth is decreasing. When I see that happening to clients who are in their eighties, I'm comforted because I know the plan will most likely succeed. However, if I notice it happening to people who are still in their sixties or seventies, I don't have a lot of confidence they can continue withdrawing at the same rate because the money is not likely to last as long as they will.

The second approach uses a similar rebalancing strategy. This approach works for people who have a variety of investments. They have large cap, small cap, growth value, and international stocks—they have a potpourri of investments. In situations like this, you or your financial planner look at the whole portfolio every six months to see how your investment allocation has changed in the last half year. You'll usually find that two or three of these investments have done better than all the others. When that happens, the best strategy is to sell off some of those winners to raise the cash for your monthly paycheck.

If selling off your winners makes you uncomfortable, go back and reread chapter 5. In that chapter, we explain the wisdom of selling off some of your winners and rebalancing your portfolio to a ratio you're comfortable with. Remember, although those winners have been good to you, they are not likely to continue earning at their current pace. Just like bushes in our yards, we need to trim the fastest growing ones a few times throughout the year to keep them looking good. Your portfolio is no different.

The third approach is what I call the bucket strategy. You essentially have three buckets. One account contains enough cash to cover ten to fifteen months of your living expenses. That's the bucket your distributions will come from. You want that cash in one of the most conservative investments you can find—such as a money market account. It's not making much money for you and probably hasn't for the last ten years due to the low Fed funds rates we've had. But you know that for the next year to fifteen months, you've got enough cash in that account to cover your monthly distributions and that the money will largely be unaffected by downturns in the stock market.

The second bucket is an account that looks out beyond that fifteen months. It has a horizon of two to four years. The money in that bucket is invested in high-quality bonds, maybe even some short-term bonds, which pay off in two to four years. When I'm filling that second bucket for clients, I'm usually looking for bonds because they can still provide returns that outpace inflation while also providing some protection from the ups and downs of the stock market. You don't want to endure that volatility if you need to withdraw in the short term.

The intermediate-term bonds I use in this bucket typically pay better than short-term bonds because the horizon is increased and the interest rate is usually higher. Generally speaking, though, the second bucket is a fixed-income portfolio of investments, and when the market is going down, you'll be using money from that second bucket to replenish the first bucket.

When the market is going up, that's when the third bucket comes into play. Bucket three holds your high-yield bond investments, your stocks, your high-dividend-paying and growth stocks. You probably have some international stocks in there as well. These are more volatile investments, but when the market is going up, which it does two-thirds to three-quarters of the time, you will be trimming from that bucket and allocating cash to bucket number one. Along the same lines, you could have all your bond interest, dividends, and capital gains distributions paid to cash and fill up your first bucket that way.

As you can see, these three approaches are all similar. What's important is how you think about it, and for many people, having those three buckets gives them a clear picture of what their investments are doing for them and where that retirement check will be coming from. This reassures them, and feeling comfortable and confident about money is an enjoyable aspect of retirement, isn't it?

Some people don't use any of the approaches I've described. These folks choose instead to live off their dividends and capital gains. Throughout the year, any dividends or capital gains from your investments are paid to cash, and the retirees sweep that money into their checking account. That way, they don't have to make decisions about what stocks to sell. However, for many retirees, their investments won't produce enough income from just dividends, bond interest, and mutual fund capital gains distributions. In these situations, it pays to have a plan for how to make up the difference. Don't leave it to chance. Think about it and know how you are going to act in different situations. Otherwise, you'll be reacting to the news you read or hear on the TV, and as we discussed earlier, we are hardwired to make the wrong decisions in times of stress in the markets.

HOW BIG DOES YOUR PAYCHECK NEED TO BE?

As I've mentioned in earlier chapters, many people assume they will be able to live on less money during retirement than they did while working. They figure that with all their big debts paid off—their house, their cars, and their children's education—that they'll be able to get by on 70 or 75 percent of what they spent before retirement.

That 70 to 75 percent estimate may be accurate for many people but not for everyone. It depends on the individual. You don't spend as much because your children are grown and you don't have them on your phone bill or car insurance bill any longer and you're not buying groceries to feed your daughters' ravenous boyfriends. But most people I've worked with find that they still want about the same income after they retire that they had before leaving the workforce.

Remember the chart I showed you in chapter 1? It's the one that shows typical preretirement spending and spending after retirement. Not long after retirement, there is usually a significant jump in spending. This is when people take an extensive trip or purchase a motor home or acquire a vacation cottage. There is a sharp spike in their spending, but in a couple of years it comes back down and levels off—usually right where it was before retirement. As people grow older and slow down, their living expenses drop off, but healthcare costs become a more significant factor. I often leave that post-retirement expense line at the same level when people reach their eighties, because that's when they need to spend more on their healthcare needs.

When I help people plan their retirement, we take into account all the potential spikes in spending. People expecting significant expenses should keep enough of their money liquid to pay for those anticipated purchases. You don't want it tied up in the stock market but rather in short-term bonds or cash so that it's available when you need it, and you aren't forced to sell stocks at a loss to pay for your expenses.

For most people, it's not difficult to figure out how much they'll need to live on. The more significant question is how you are going to utilize your assets to make that paycheck. Have you saved and invested enough to complement your Social Security or pension payments? Your goal should be to take enough out of your investments to provide a steady income stream while maintaining an account balance large enough to ensure the income keeps flowing for as long as you are alive.

The rule of thumb is that you can keep those account balances high enough for sustained withdrawals for the rest of your life if you limit those annual withdrawals to about

4 percent of the total in the accounts. If you've saved a significant amount of money or you are a wildly successful investor, you might be able to take out more, but an initial 4 percent withdrawal rate is a very good gauge to use. Take out much more than that, odds are your retirement scenario won't be successful. Take out much less and you'll have to decide where you want the money to go after you pass away. A crucial question, however, is whether that 4 percent is enough for you to live on. Another factor to consider is inflation. Many retirees using the 4 percent rule will increase their withdrawals by a small amount each year to match the Federal Reserve's target inflation rate. That is fine because inflation increases are built into that initial 4 percent withdrawal rate.

It's important to note that this isn't a set-it-and-forget-it approach. You'll need to continue to monitor your plan throughout retirement to make sure your spending habits are sustainable for the long term.

IF YOU COME UP SHORT

Many people close to retirement who add up their Social Security benefits, pension payments, and retirement account distributions find they will not have enough retirement income to cover all their expenses in retirement. Maybe they lost a lot during the Great Recession and were never able to build their investments back up.

Perhaps they decided to pay for all of their children's college education so their children weren't saddled with $50,000 in debt before they got their first job. Maybe they miscalculated and thought Social Security was going to save them. Whatever the reason, they are nearing retirement, and they just don't have enough money to cover their living expenses if they were to quit working as soon as they hoped.

Unfortunately, there are a lot of Americans in this predicament. There are a million studies out there, but most of them offer the same grim conclusions: Americans aren't very good at saving for retirement. Less than half of the American workers who are employed by a company with a 401(k) retirement plan contribute to the account, and a report from the Economic Policy Institute in 2016 found that the median retirement savings for families aged fifty-six to sixty-one was $17,000. This means that for most Americans, Social Security will be their entire retirement income.

Your situation may not be that dire, but you may still have some doubts about whether you saved enough. If you're close to retirement and your rough calculations show that you, too, may come up short, you have a few options:

- Save more, starting right now.
- Spend less.

- Work longer.
- Get a part-time job in retirement.
- Try to get a higher return on the investments that you do have.

As a financial planner, I find that last option is a little scary. As we've already mentioned, you can't predict what the stock market will do. We could go through a ten-year period like the first decade of this century—after the dot-com bubble burst—when we had meager returns. And the sequence of those returns has an enormous impact on the health of your portfolio.

Here's an example of what I'm talking about:

Say you had $1 million in your portfolio and you plan to withdraw $90,000 a year of that during your retirement. Let's look at what happens to that million-dollar portfolio under two different scenarios.

The first scenario (the left-hand column in the chart below) looks at how that portfolio would perform from 1995 to 2015 according to the actual rate of return of the Dow Jones Industrial Average (DJIA) during that twenty-year period. The right-hand column looks at how that portfolio would perform if the annual rate for that twenty-year period was reversed.

The Effect of the Sequence of Returns

Beginning balance: $1,000,000
Withdrawal per year: $90,000

Dow Jones Historical Returns		Year	Dow Jones Reverse Historical Returns	
Rate of Return	Year End Balance		Rate of Return	Year End Balance
33.45%	$1,244,520	1995	−2.23%	$887,670
26.01%	$1,478.269	1996	7.52%	$864,414
22.64%	$1,722,964	1997	26.50%	$1,003,475
16.10%	$1,910,344	1998	7.26%	$986,297
25.22%	$2,302,152	1999	5.53%	$950,820
−6.17%	$2,070,156	2000	11.02%	$965,628
−7.10%	$1,833,092	2001	18.82%	$1,057,350
−16.76%	$1,435,811	2002	−33.84%	$609,575
25.32%	$1,709,387	2003	6.43%	$558,782
3.15%	$1,673,198	2004	16.29%	$559,797
−0.61%	$1,573,025	2005	−0.61%	$466,693
16.29%	$1,739,239	2006	3.15%	$391,075
6.43%	$1,761,107	2007	25.32%	$400,103
−33.84%	$1,075,201	2008	−16.76%	$243,034
18.82%	$1,187,544	2009	−7.10%	$135,769
11.02%	$1,288,446	2010	−6.17%	$37,395
5.53%	$1,206,355	2011	25.22%	$0
7.26%	$1,203,900	2012	16.10%	$0
26.50%	$1,432,922	2013	22.64%	$0
7.52%	$1,450,663	2014	26.01%	$0
−2.23%	$1,328,270	2015	33.45%	$0

Average Rate of Return: 8.79%	Average Rate of Return: 8.79%
Ending Balance: $1,328,270	Ending Balance: $0

As you can see, the value of this portfolio in the left-hand column continued to grow throughout the twenty years, even as the investor withdrew $90,000 a year for retirement, which is significantly more than the 4 percent amount I discussed a few pages ago. The year-end balances go up and down as you would expect them to as the market goes up and down, but after twenty years, the portfolio has nevertheless gone up by more than $300,000. Not bad!

Now let's look at what would happen if those annual stock market rates of return were reversed. The return for 1995 is the actual return from 2015, the return for 1996 is for 2014, and so on. The overall rate of return for the twenty years is the same (8.79 percent), but each year is different. What happens to the portfolio when we do this?

Whoa! This outcome is dramatically different! As you can see, that million-dollar portfolio quickly declines and is completely drained by 2011.

The point here is not to scare you but to drive home the fact that you can't expect the stock market to always cooperate with you when you are chasing a higher rate of return. You may just be at the beginning of a low-return environment in the market.

Investors call this phenomenon that I've illustrated here "sequence of return risk" or "sequence risk," and it's a major concern for retirees who are living off the proceeds of their investments. When you retire—and whether you retire during a bull market or during a bear market—can have an enormous impact on your portfolio. Two people with identical portfolios can have dramatically different results depending on the state of the economy when they start their retirement.

Say you retire at the bottom of a bear market (think back to the period from October 2007 to March 2009); the prices for your holdings were low, and instead of investing money in the stock market to take advantage of the low prices, you sold equities to pay for your retirement. As a result, you have fewer shares of equities with which to take advantage of the upturn that follows.

Compare that to someone who retires when stock prices are high. You don't have to sell as many shares of equities to make your retirement paycheck, and this leaves you a stronger portfolio that will continue earning for you long into your retirement.

Some of this clearly falls into the category of sheer luck. If you happen to retire when your portfolio is flush, and stock prices remain high for several years in the beginning of your retirement, you are one of the lucky ones. If things aren't looking so good, however, you might want to delay your retirement for a time or consider spending a little less for a few years initially.

However, there are other ways to manage sequence risk. Having a globally diversified portfolio with investments in stocks, bonds, and cash is one way to avoid selling your stocks at depressed prices. You can also adjust your 4 percent withdrawal rate, temporarily lowering your withdrawals to minimize the damage to your overall portfolio. Or you could forgo inflation adjustments to your withdrawal rate for a few years. Regardless of your situation, it's wise to go into retirement with the understanding that your paycheck may need to fluctuate according to the stock market environment at the time.

WORKING FOR YOUR RETIREMENT PAYCHECK

You can also consider working part time for a while if you find yourself in a bear market early in your retirement. Many people are taking this route and finding it rewarding. Even some people who don't need to work enjoy working; it keeps them active and fit or gets them out in the community. Here are some options to consider:

- Negotiate with your current employer to scale back your hours and continue working, either as a subcontractor or as a consultant.
- Monetize your hobby. You may love woodworking, for instance, and find that people are willing to pay top dollar for your elegantly dovetailed jewelry boxes.
- Start a new career. Some professionals—teachers, writers, designers, and IT professionals, for instance—

find post-retirement jobs with nonprofit groups. These organizations don't usually pay much, but if you believe in their mission, working for them might have rewards beyond a paycheck.

Regardless of how you do it, having a little extra income in your early years of retirement will be beneficial later. The work doesn't need to be as hard or as stressful as a full-time career position. I recently had a conversation with a bartender in Palm Springs while there on vacation. He retired from one of the big investment banks on Wall Street as a corporate attorney. He had way more money than he needed, but he still took a job bartending a couple of days a week. He loved it. It got him out of the house and doing something different. "I learned you can't play golf every day in retirement," he said. And since he worked for a large hotel chain, he was able to capitalize on the reduced rates at hotels around the world, such as paying $13 a night in downtown Paris for a week. If you make your part-time retirement job fun, you'll enjoy doing it and it won't feel like work.

MISTAKES TO AVOID

The stock market, as we've seen in this chapter and earlier ones, is dependable in the long run but extremely unpredictable in the short term. If you plan on living off the proceeds from your investments in retirement, it pays to learn as much as you can about how it works and what you can expect from it.

For example, it's a mistake to focus on dividends and not total returns. Dividends and capital gains both feed into total returns, and capital gains can be much more substantial than dividends. Many high-dividend-paying companies are paying you to hold their stock, because many of them grow very slowly and won't have the large capital gains like a high-growth technology company. Think about how fast your local energy company is growing compared to Amazon. Odds are, your local energy company pays dividends to encourage people to hold their stock, while Amazon doesn't need to do so and can use stockholders' cash to invest in the company instead of paying it out to shareholders. Focusing too much on just those dividend payments may divert your attention from opportunities with other stocks that are making significant capital gains.

The other mistake people make has to do with planning. If there is one message you get from this discussion about your retirement paycheck, I hope it's this: plan carefully and follow the plan.

You know it's a mistake to go grocery shopping when you're hungry and you don't have a list of specific items to buy, right? You don't want to find yourself wandering the aisles throwing random, tasty-looking treats in your shopping cart. You make rash decisions and come home with a lot of things you wouldn't have bought if you prepared a list before going to the store. You only want to buy what you need, and you want to avoid sudden, impulsive purchases.

Behave this way in retirement. You can't be haphazard about how much you spend each month. You can't afford to have highly variable expenses based on whims or fleeting wishes. If your retirement plan is going to work, you have to have a long-term perspective on what your spending needs will be and have a plan to cover those needs.

Following a careful plan and adjusting portfolio withdrawals according to what the market is doing is also a vital aspect of our next topic: "Passing on Your Assets." Estate planning goes hand in hand with retirement planning, so let's move on to the next chapter and find out how to best do that.

CHAPTER 8

PASSING ON YOUR ASSETS

Harry Houdini was a masterful escape artist, climbing out of the ground after being buried alive and finding a way out of a straitjacket while trapped underwater. Unfortunately, Houdini could not escape death, but he found a way to keep his name alive even after he passed by promising his wife, Bess, that he would contact her from the afterlife and by stating in his will that a séance should be held every year on the anniversary of his death.

History is full of fascinating wills—there are stories of people leaving fortunes to their pets or stipulating where their ashes will be scattered (Gene Roddenberry, the creator of *Star Trek*, had his ashes scattered from a space satellite)—but for most of us, estate planning involves making sure our possessions and money are distributed to the right people as quickly and as easily as possible.

Estate planning is an emotional subject for many people. It involves the eventual death of a loved one—something no one wants to think about—and it often generates a sense of guilt on the part of family members who gain wealth when someone they love dies. Consequently, most people don't like to talk about it. (Houdini, for example, apparently wanted to put off some of his conversations with his wife until he was enjoying the afterlife.)

However, estate planning is something everyone needs to address. If you don't, you are leaving your wishes up to politicians (state or federal) to make the decisions for you since they are the individuals who make up state and federal laws. A clear will can bring you the peace of mind of knowing your hard-earned wealth will continue to help those you love. To help you through that, we'll discuss some of the best strategies for distributing your estate, whether it's with a will or trust, what kind of documents you should have in place before you pass, and how to find a knowledgeable and experienced attorney to help you.

GETTING STARTED

Estate planning is a simple matter for many people who merely want to pass on their assets to their surviving spouse or children. Although I always recommend clients find a good estate attorney, those with simple estates can often use online services to set up their will. You do everything yourself and fill out the documents online, and when you're done, the online company sends you your documents, you sign them, and you're finished. It's much cheaper than hiring an attorney, but you don't get an attorney to guide you through the process to ensure your documents are conforming with your wishes.

Other estates are more complex. These folks may have intricate business interests or complicated families. They may have had several marriages and divorces, and they may have several children, including adopted children and stepchildren. If you are the patriarch of a large family and you have vast wealth, you will need help structuring your estate. Let's say your son and daughter-in-law are happily married at the time you pass away and you've left him everything in your estate. Then ten years down the road, he goes through a divorce. That means half of your assets will go to someone who is no longer in your family. An attorney can help you find ways to protect your wealth and ensure that it goes to (and stays with!) the people you want to inherit those assets.

WHY YOU SHOULD PLAN YOUR ESTATE

Estate planning is crucial because if you don't do it, the

government will step in and do it for you. And the government may not do it the way you would have wanted. I knew a man who was divorced and remarried. He died without a will. The state probate court gave all his assets to his second wife, and the children from his first marriage received nothing. I doubt this was what he would have wanted, but it was too late for him to do anything about it.

This story highlights why you need a sound, legal plan to ensure your expectations and intentions are met after you pass away. Since all estates are subject to probate proceedings, it's crucial that you have the correct paperwork ahead of time. Without a will or some other safeguard, your estate will be considered "intestate," and a probate judge will make decisions about who gets paid what and who gets paid first. The court can even make decisions about child guardianship.

Not all estates are probated, however. If your estate is below a certain threshold—for some states that limit is $75,000 and in other states it is higher—your survivors must file a small estate affidavit that details your assets and debts and shows how those debts have been paid and where the remainder of the assets have been allocated. That's it. You don't have to go through the entire probate process.

DOCUMENTS FOR ESTATE PLANNING

I always look at sound estate planning as one of the greatest gifts you can give to your family after you're gone. If you have it set up correctly, it makes life so much easier for whoever is left behind. Regardless of the size of your estate, a minimum protection strategy should include the following steps and documents:

- Properly titled accounts
- Will(s)—one for each spouse if married
- Durable power of attorney for property and healthcare
- Living will or healthcare proxy
- Up-to-date beneficiary designations
- Letter of intent
- Guardianship designations
- Possibly a living trust

Properly titling your accounts is one of the simplest actions to take when developing an estate plan. But even though it's simple, many people overlook this important step. Just titling an account jointly with your spouse can ensure they have access to those funds if you pass away. Titling is estate planning. Here is a quick rundown of the ways you can title your nonretirement accounts (checking, savings, brokerage, etc.):

- **Individually.** The account is in your name only and

its contents will transfer based on the language in your will. If individual assets are large enough, they will need to go through probate.

- **Joint Tenants with Rights of Survivorship (JTWROS).** The most common way married couples title assets. All assets pass to the surviving account holder, and JTWROS supersedes any language in your will.

- **Tenants in Common.** Recommended choice for unmarried couples or those with shared accounts. While the account holders are alive, it is owned by the holders in proportion to the amount they contributed to the account. When one of the account holders dies, his interest will pass to whomever he has specified in his will.

- **Payable on Death (POD)/Transfer on Death.** This acts much like a beneficiary designation. It is a way to provide beneficiary designations to accounts that don't normally have beneficiaries associated with them.

A will can be a simple document, but it is the foundation of your estate plan. It spells out how you want your assets distributed. It may also name a guardian for your children if they are still young, and it names an executor for your estate. An executor is a person responsible for carrying out each provision of your will. This person can be your spouse, an adult offspring, or someone else you trust to do the job right. Often, the executor is your attorney.

When estate assets are to be inherited by a minor child or an adult who is not capable of managing the responsibilities that accompany a sudden increase in wealth (spendthrift), a trust can be set up by your will. The trust names a trustee to help manage the trust assets and distribute the funds to the trust beneficiary according to the guidelines set up in the trust document. Oftentimes, these distribution rules provide for a beneficiary's particular needs—education or health maintenance, for instance—so it's not locked up when an heir needs those funds for something. A trust can also set up rules about distributions that control how, when, and under what circumstances trust assets are distributed for a beneficiary. Does the beneficiary need money to buy a car? Yes. A Porsche? No.

I don't mean to sound facetious, but when you have a will drawn up, make sure you sign it. You wouldn't believe how often people go to the trouble of having a detailed will drawn up but never take the simple step of signing it.

A durable power of attorney for property provides explicit instructions to your family and to the courts spelling out who has the legal authority to act in your place for legal and financial affairs should you become incapacitated but not deceased. This document is sometimes set up to serve two purposes—to designate someone to oversee your finances and a second to monitor your healthcare—but often, they are two different documents. That's how we'll discuss them.

The durable power of attorney for property designates someone to manage your financial affairs when you are incapacitated. They can sign your tax return, pay your mortgage, and even use your checking account to pay your bills, although banks are making that increasingly difficult to do. People usually give their spouse power of attorney, but it can also be your lawyer, accountant, or brother-in-law. You have to get confirmation that these folks are willing and able to take on the responsibility.

In the event someone needs to step in and manage your affairs for you, it's important to note that all institutions will do a complete legal review of the documents. Given our litigious environment, companies are much more rigorous in the use of these documents because they want to make sure they are doing everything appropriately. For example, when you check into a hospital, the facility will usually ask you to fill out its own power-of-attorney form.

A durable power of attorney for healthcare or advance directive gives someone power to make your healthcare decisions for you when you can't. They interact with your doctors to decide the type of care you need. A **living will**, on the other hand, provides your overall wishes to the doctors and nurses who are caring for you when you are incapacitated. These documents usually say something like, "When Bob was in a good frame of mind, he said he doesn't want a hospital or doctor to take extraordinary lifesaving measures to continue his life."

A living will allows you to reject life-sustaining medical intervention when you are incapacitated by a terminal illness. A living will can also stipulate that you want all forms of life support given to you. This is a great document for your loved ones because it takes some decisions out of their hands and doesn't cause them undue anxiety when end-of-life care decisions are made. You will have essentially told them that it is OK to stop providing care. Just like all things related to estate planning, you are making it easier on your loved ones at a very difficult time. Again, you should set this up when you get your will drawn up.

Up-to-date beneficiary designations are a critical piece to a properly established estate plan, and this simple step is often overlooked. Beneficiary designations are important legal forms that should be up to date and on file for all your employer retirement plans, your personal IRAs, life insurance policies, and annuities.

Beneficiary designations trump the instructions you have in your will. If your will states that your retirement account should go to your spouse, but the retirement account has someone else named as the beneficiary of the account, the assets will flow to the account beneficiary and not the person named in your will. For example, say you are divorced and have remarried. If you update your will to take care of your second spouse when you pass but fail to remove your first spouse as the beneficiary on your retirement account or life insurance policy, the assets in that account will automatically go to your first spouse. The devil is in the details on these things, and you need to make sure *all of your beneficiary designations are up to date.*

A **letter of intent** is like a living will because it provides additional information to those who will step in to manage your needs. However, it is not related to healthcare. It has no legal authority and doesn't bind your heirs to doing anything specific. It is usually a more personal and descriptive document for how to handle some aspects of your financial affairs and belongings.

Unlike a will, you don't have to pass away before this document can become useful. If you are in the hospital for an extended period, or even out of the country and unable to manage your affairs, a letter of intent is a useful guide to those you rely on for help.

A letter of intent can include any of the following:

- Thorough listing of all your nonfinancial assets (house, cars, jewelry, art, collectibles, etc.).
- Location of all your legal documents (will, trust, titles, deeds to property, tax returns, account statements, businesses or partnerships, etc.).
- Personal information and documents (Social Security number, birth certificate, divorce and/or citizenship papers).
- Location of keys and safe deposit boxes.
- Passwords, PINs, and account numbers of all your financial accounts (banks, credit cards, brokerage accounts, etc.).
- Login information for all your email, social media, websites, etc.
- Contact information for your trusted advisors (financial planner, attorney, insurance provider, accountant, etc.).
- If not included in your will or trust, you can provide the names of anyone you would like to receive certain possessions of yours.
- The name of any charities that you support and would like donations to go to in lieu of flowers at your funeral.
- Names and contact information for any person or organization that may be a beneficiary of your estate.
- Instructions for any person or pet that you provided care for.

A letter of intent can include a lot of information. It can be a step-by-step guide for your executor and will save an enormous amount of time and energy. Having all of the pertinent information gathered in one document will eliminate the need for your loved ones to be searching through desk drawers or file cabinets in an attempt to cobble together all the pieces of your financial life. This also eliminates the risk that your loved ones miss a critical piece of information about an asset or benefit that they didn't know existed.

Guardianship designation for a child or another adult is a straightforward document. You give someone else the legal right to become that child's or adult's guardian for their property and living needs in the event you pass away. For most people, this is a trusted relative or friend. Make sure whoever you identify knows about it in advance.

If a couple is unmarried but have a lifelong dedication to each other, providing a guardianship designation is one way to ensure the most appropriate person will care for you in a time of need.

ADVANTAGES OF A TRUST

Depending on your individual situation, utilizing a living trust for your estate plan can make a lot of sense. **A living trust or revocable trust** is when you take assets out of your name and place them under a trust document. It's a trust account with your Social Security number on it, but you don't "individually own" the asset anymore; you are the trustee of the account.

You can take money out of it, put money into it, and you pay income taxes on money you earn from this trust account. The trust can be a cash account or a portfolio of different investments. Your house can be in the trust. Throughout your lifetime, you can make any adjustments to the trust document, which is why it is called a revocable trust.

You can also move assets into and out of the trust at any time while living. However, when you pass away, that trust becomes an irrevocable trust. It becomes a separate entity with its own tax identification number, and it files its own tax return every year. Your successor trustee named in the trust document becomes the person who is legally required to adhere to the language and instructions that are in the trust document. The successor trustee can be a trusted family member (spouse, sibling, child) or close personal friend. Sometimes a corporate trustee can be named. Whoever it is must comply with the instructions you have laid out in the original trust language.

Creating a trust allows you to avoid the cost and delays of probate. If you and your spouse die, your successor trustee takes over the trust account and manages the assets and distributes the funds according to how you've set up the trust. Nothing titled in the trust needs to go through probate because it is not titled in your individual name.

Here's an example of the provisions you might have in a revocable trust. Say you set up the trust to provide for your spouse during her lifetime. When she passes, the assets in the trust should go to your three sons. The account's funds can be professionally managed and invested throughout your spouse's lifetime while the money is distributed as needed for her living and healthcare needs.

Say your children are young and you don't want them to receive a large inheritance before they are able to handle the responsibility of managing it appropriately. So you include a stipulation that the trust assets should not pass to your sons until they reach the age of thirty-five. This means that when the first son reaches the age of thirty-five, he gets a third of what's in the trust account. When the second son reaches thirty-five, he receives half of what's left. The final portion is distributed when the third son reaches thirty-five.

After the assets in the trust are fully distributed, the trust is dissolved because it has served its purpose, which was to have someone knowledgeable manage its day-to-day affairs until your wealth is transferred to your children at the appropriate time.

This is a fast and easy process, and it keeps your estate out of the probate courts and ensures your personal and business affairs remain private. You can move as many assets as you want into that trust. Doing so can ensure your individual assets are beneath the probate threshold in your state. When you do that, many states require you to file only a small estate affidavit, which we discussed earlier, and keeps your estate out of probate altogether.

Many people like knowing that their wealth will be distributed in a simplified and direct way after they die. Things aren't tied up, and it's simple for a new trustee to come in and take over management of the trust. A trust doesn't mean you won't need a will and some of these other documents. It is an additional document that complements the other estate planning documents and steps you have taken. I personally set up a revocable trust for my wife and children because I've seen how simple and easy it is for your assets to pass on after you die.

A revocable trust is an effective estate planning tool that can allow you to avoid probate and distribute your assets according to your wishes. However, much like a will, the document doesn't have any effect if you don't sign it *and* change the title of your assets to the name of the trust. Assets are only governed by the trust document if they are titled in the name of the trust. If you were to forget to change the title of your house or an investment account, those assets may have to go through probate and would not be governed or distributed according to your directives in the trust. It is a simple step that is often overlooked. So make sure you sign the document and retitle your assets.

GIFTING STRATEGIES

Thanks to the recent changes in estate tax law, most people no longer worry about the federal estate tax. In 2019, anyone who dies has a lifetime gift and estate tax exemption of $11.4 million. This means you can pass on up to $11.4 million without owing any federal tax. In future years, the amount increases to adjust for inflation.

Married couples can coordinate their estates in order to pass on up to twice that amount. However, due to sunset clauses in the tax law, the exemption amount will revert back to the 2017 level of $5.6 million per individual. This merely describes what happens at the federal level and does not take into account estate taxes levied by individual states.

If you do think your estate might owe estate tax due to federal or state tax law, one way to avoid or reduce the tax bill is to give away assets throughout your lifetime. In 2019, you can make an unlimited number of $15,000 gifts, tax-free each calendar year. These gifts are called annual exclusion gifts. By taking advantage of this provision in the law, you can reduce the potential size of your estate by making $15,000 gifts each year to as many people as you wish.

A married couple can double that amount to $30,000 because each of you can make a gift to the same person. For instance, say you have a married son. You and your wife can transfer up to $60,000 to him and his wife ($30,000 to your son and $30,000 to your daughter-in-law). Over a ten-year period, that would equate to passing on $600,000 completely tax-free. If you have more children or grandchildren, you can imagine the amount of wealth you can transfer free of estate taxes. And even if you aren't concerned about the estate tax, gifts also provide you the benefit of seeing the joy the recipients have for receiving your gifts to them during your lifetime.

Again, the central goal of estate planning is the quick and efficient transfer of your assets to whom you want them to go to after you pass away. To do this, make sure all your financial accounts are titled appropriately, have clear beneficiary designations, and that you review those and update them as circumstances change. Who will own your checking and savings account? Whom will your home transfer to when you die? Setting these things up before your death will ensure your desires are achieved.

ISSUES THAT COMPLICATE THINGS

Life can get messy sometimes, and when it does, your estate can become tangled. That means you have to take special care when planning how your assets will be distributed. Here are some circumstances that can complicate your estate planning:

- You've been married more than once.
- You own a business or are involved in a partnership.
- You own real estate in more than one state.
- You are caring for a disabled child or family member.
- You have minor children, a problem child, or you don't have any children at all.
- You want to donate all or part of your estate to a charity.
- You have substantial assets locked in 401(k) accounts and IRAs.
- Your spouse recently died.
- You're recently divorced, and you haven't updated your estate plan.
- You have a sizable estate that could be affected by federal and state taxes.

If you fall into any of these situations, I advise finding

a good estate planning attorney to help you. You would never want to use an online service for a complicated estate. You should not be doing this yourself, because the legal and tax ramifications can cost you much, much more than the costs for obtaining legal help.

It's also essential that you investigate your state's laws concerning estate taxes. Although the federal government has raised the limit for when you have to pay estate taxes (often called the "death tax" by politicians) to $11.4 million, not all states have moved in lockstep with the federal government on this issue. Some have kept the threshold much lower, and in those states, you must design your estate documents to accommodate state law rather than federal law.

For example, Oregon's estate tax kicks in for any estate over $1 million, and the tax ranges from 10 to 16 percent. Surviving spouses usually don't have to pay federal or state estate taxes. It's when the assets transfer outside of marriage, such as going to your children, that estate taxes come into play.

Your estate has to pay federal estate taxes when the estate's combined gross assets and prior taxable gifts exceed $11.4 million. That threshold used to be much lower, but in recent years, the federal government has increased it. In 2016, the limit was $5.45 million, and not that long ago, the threshold was $1 million. Anything above this amount was taxed at a rate around 50 percent.

Estate taxes are paid before beneficiaries receive their inheritance, but inheritance taxes apply to assets after they've been passed down. There is no federal inheritance tax, but a handful of states still levy one.

When you are doing sound estate planning, you can also set up provisions that ease your mind by anticipating future problems. Family dynamics can undoubtedly enter the picture. If you have an adult child who seems to run into financial or legal difficulties, for instance, you can set up a trust in such a way that the trust is not considered that child's asset and, as such, can't be tapped or drained if the child goes into bankruptcy or is sued by a business associate. If that type of scenario is a concern, you could protect your estate from creditors.

Some of these issues are what I call "the ghost around the corner." They may not be issues at all. And the probability of them happening are extremely small. But individuals can imagine some unfortunate situations happening down the road, so they set up provisions for them. Sometimes these ideas can get out of hand. We can't cover *every* possible scenario and have to recognize that at some point we will need to trust others. Covering every possible scenario is like buying insurance for every conceivable mishap. In these situations, it always helps to get advice from an attorney first.

FINDING AN ATTORNEY

If your situation includes two or more examples of the circumstances I listed in the previous section, you should consider getting a skilled and experienced estate planning attorney. You should be looking for someone who specializes in this field and not someone who dabbles in it when there aren't other cases to pursue.

Here are some factors to consider when selecting an attorney:

- How many years of experience in estate planning does the attorney have?
- Will you be working directly with the attorney or will your case be assigned to a paralegal and the work later reviewed by the attorney?
- How long does the attorney's process take?
- If you are setting up a revocable trust, will the attorney help you set up the funding for the trust? In other words, is it part of the agreement that they will retitle any assets, such as your house, that you want to include in the trust? You want someone who is familiar with the process and will help you file the right documents with the county clerk.

- How are updates to your estate handled—will the attorney reach out to you or are you required to monitor it and set up future appointments?
- Does this attorney stay on top of tax laws and estate law changes? In one state I'm familiar with, a judge ten or fifteen years ago ruled that all pages of a will or trust must be initialed by the person, thus voiding all the trust documents that had been created up to that point throughout the state. Will your attorney be on top of situations like that?
- Does the attorney's personality suit you? Can you see yourself working with this person and sharing personal information?
- Does the attorney charge a flat fee or is it by the hour? For most estate planning engagements, attorneys charge a flat fee. But certain situations may call for an hourly charge. At what point would an hourly charge begin?
- Has the attorney designated someone to take over their cases in the event they retire or are incapacitated themselves?
- Is the attorney available to advise you on other matters? Is this going to be your go-to attorney for other legal issues you encounter in life, and if so, what resources do they bring to the relationship for these ancillary issues?
- These are not all the questions you may want to ask an attorney. But receiving answers to the above

questions will go a long way toward making you feel satisfied you are working with a good one and one whom you are comfortable with.

SPECIAL CIRCUMSTANCES

When I began telling people I was writing this book, many said they were very interested in the topic of retirement because they have young children. This surprised me a little because this is a book about retirement. But then I realized how important it is to parents to know there is a plan in place for their offspring in the event the parent dies prematurely. It's equally important to grandparents because they can see their life's legacy continuing on through their grandchildren's lives.

For example, say you have a disabled child, and that child grows into an adult. They are receiving help—training, therapy, day care, and benefits—but then suddenly, you and your spouse die and all your assets go to this adult child. The wealth precludes them from receiving any more state aid. Ironically, although the disabled person now has some wealth, he is losing the framework for his life. He might be losing his therapy, job, job training, or skilled care, and his life will be worse because of that. What's more, the child's needs are such that he will quickly drain his inheritance.

This scenario leads to the question of what's best for the

child. Some people will see the value of that child continuing to receive state aid, while others might feel they shouldn't take any state aid if they can afford privately paid help. Again, these are some special circumstances that you have to put some thought to if you have a child with special needs and you're planning your retirement. If the adult child's individual needs are best served by not providing them with an inheritance so he can continue to receive state aid, talk to your attorney and make sure your plan follows your desires.

Your children from previous marriages also need to be carefully considered. You may have remarried and raised other children, but you feel strongly that your own offspring should benefit from your assets. You must take steps to ensure this happens. Check your beneficiary statements and ensure your children are remembered in your will and/or trust documents. You don't want your only direct descendants to come away from your death with nothing.

By the same token, you may find it worthwhile to acknowledge a child's poor financial habits. If you feel they aren't responsible enough at the age of eighteen for a large inheritance—such as if they are inclined to hit the road as a rock band devotee—spendthrift provisions in revocable trusts can be set up to ensure they don't waste their inheritance buying Jell-O shots at Phish concerts.

Remember, estate planning doesn't have to be complicated, but it's something everyone should take care of. A strong estate plan will ensure that your wishes are carried out after you pass. This should bring both you and your heirs peace of mind.

CHAPTER 9

TURNING THEORY
INTO REALITY

If you've reached this point in the book, you should feel good about taking this big step into retirement. Whether that step is in the next couple of years or decades into the future, I hope I've given you a lot to do and think about.

Earlier in the book we talked about the real fear some people feel when they contemplate retirement—we compared retirement to a bear that's been locked in the closet—but I hope you're feeling less apprehension now that we've had a chance to talk through some of the challenges (and rewards) that you'll encounter when you leave the workforce and start writing your own paycheck.

At this point, you should have a much better handle on

the realities of retirement. You know how to assess your current financial situation, and you may have spent some time contemplating your goals for when you retire. You have a better understanding of what you can expect from the government—in the way of benefits as well as taxes—and I hope you are more comfortable with the uncertainties of the stock market. In short, I hope I've eased your mind.

If you're on the verge of retirement, you no doubt now have a better idea of how much of a retirement you can afford. If you're still ten or fifteen years away from retirement, you might be looking for ways to tighten your belt so you can save more for when the time comes. If you're just starting your journey toward retirement, I hope I've convinced you of the importance of saving early and often.

DON'T GO IT ALONE

Wherever you land across this spectrum, a central question for you is this: Will you go it alone or will you look for a trusted advisor to help you navigate these financial straits? I hope it's the latter. I know it's self-serving for me to advocate that—I am a financial planner, after all—but I also know from experience that retirees who find the right planner do significantly better preparing for and enjoying their retirement when they have an expert on their team.

To understand the types of professionals you have to choose from, it helps to know that all financial advisors fall into one of two broad categories: (1) Registered Investment Advisors (RIAs) and (2) broker-dealers.

RIAs are registered with the Securities and Exchange Commission (SEC) or their state securities' regulator. Most brokers are members of the Financial Industry Regulatory Authority (FINRA), which is regulated under the Securities and Exchange Act of 1934.

Brokers are held to what's referred to as the suitability standard when providing financial and investment advice, rather than the strict fiduciary standard that RIAs must meet. This means that a broker's advice must be "suitable" for the client's needs at that particular time. This suitability standard is far less stringent than the fiduciary standard where an RIA must make recommendations that are in the client's best interest.

In addition to the fiduciary obligation, the other main difference between an RIA and a broker is in the way they are compensated. RIAs either charge their clients a percentage of assets under management or a fixed fee. Brokers, in contrast, receive compensation from commissions they receive on the investment products they recommend and sell.

This is where a CERTIFIED FINANCIAL PLANNER™

professional can come aboard and help. Good financial planners, particularly Fee-Only advisors who don't earn commissions by selling you certain products, have your best interests in mind. While an investment advisor helps you pick stocks and bonds, financial planners take a broad view of your financial landscape. They understand the stock market and will help you build a balanced and sustainable portfolio. They can also advise you on managing debts, determining the best time to retire, and planning for your estate. They aren't trying to sell you any products so they can earn a commission. They want to protect and build your investments, and they have a fiduciary and legal responsibility to put your interests first.

A 2018 study in the *Journal of Consumer Research* found that the key to your sense of well-being is feeling reassured about both your current economic situation and your future financial prospects. The satisfaction you get from your financial well-being is as important as job satisfaction, a stable relationship, and physical health *combined*, the study found. Having someone help you deal with your finances can be "transformative—like having an anvil removed from your back," financial planner Jill Schlesinger told the *New York Times* when the study came out.

People who work with a coach or a financial advisor make better decisions, increase their wealth, and have a much happier and contented retirement compared to those struggling alone to keep their boat upright and on course.

A Fee-Only financial planner is someone you want on your side. They typically earn about 1 percent of the total amount of the assets they manage, and they have a fiduciary responsibility to work in your best interests. While some financial planners do earn commissions on certain products they sell, I don't take that approach. To me, it sets up a conflict of interest; something may be profitable for me but not necessarily a wise investment for the client, and I don't want to put myself in a situation where I have to choose. Consequently, I've set up my practice so that we are on the same team. In the end, you want someone who is always looking for what is best for you.

Finding someone who will work solely in your best interest can be a challenge, however. There are a lot of different financial professionals in the world, and many financial advisors cloak themselves as financial planners. In reality, these advisors are trying to sell you insurance products or some other commercial product. That is where their focus is; they may not be interested in spending time talking about all the different aspects of your life, just the areas where they have a product to sell to you.

Fee-Only RIAs who hold the CERTIFIED FINANCIAL PLANNER™ certification have a fiduciary responsibility to you. What's more, they take a much more holistic view of your financial situation and the many aspects of your life that affect it. They aren't going to micromanage your securities, buying and selling every hour of every day and firing off text messages with tips on the hot, new stock. They aren't going to promise a specific return or suggest that they will outperform the market. You cannot believe anyone who promises that. The stock market is too unpredictable. If anyone tells you they know what is going to happen in the future, run away. No one knows exactly what is going to happen. If they did, they'd probably be on an island in the Caribbean (probably their own island)!

Instead, a financial planner builds a customized investment plan that takes into account your tolerance for risk as well as your goals for your money. A planner looks to minimize fees and tax impacts and keeps your portfolio balanced. A planner counsels you on those big-ticket items, such as how to pay for college or how to set up your estate. They can advise you on charitable giving, insurance, or business-continuation planning, and they will make sure your assets are wisely distributed between taxable and tax-advantaged accounts. They'll help you set up your retirement paycheck with withdrawals that make the most sense.

Are financial planners a good investment? While you should be suspicious of any financial planner who promises to deliver specific returns, some experts say you could add about 3 percent in returns to your portfolio by using a financial planner who manages your assets with discipline and care rather than taking the do-it-yourself approach.

A white paper report from Vanguard found that financial planners who follow the philosophies we've outlined in this book add value at all stages of your portfolio management, from allocating your assets across a diversified spectrum to withdrawing funds for retirement. According to Vanguard and other academic studies, a financial planner's most significant value is when we help our clients modulate their behavior when the stock market is either tanking or soaring. It's times like those that investors often chuck their plan out the window and do some crazy things, such as selling all their stock when the market is at its nadir, or pouring cash into it when stock prices are high. A financial planner helps you keep things in perspective when the world looks crazy, and studies show this kind of "behavioral coaching" alone can add 1 to 2 percent in returns.

Having a client-centered advisor is like having a trusted advisor help you buy a car. The advisor doesn't care whether you buy a Toyota or a Ford; they are impartial, objective, and focused on the pros and cons of each and help you reach your own decision. What's more, an advisor doesn't have an emotional attachment to, say, the color blue. You might fall in love with a car because it's a shade of blue that you love, but the advisor would be there to remind you that the blue car gets far worse gas mileage than the white one and doesn't have as good of a safety rating.

I often tell my clients that I am the insurance policy that protects them against themselves. People who go it alone are often impulsive and make reactive financial decisions based on emotion. These are almost always the wrong decisions, and I consider it my job to explain why. A good financial planner brings experience, perspective, and data into the discussion, and we use those tools to help keep people on track.

WHAT TO LOOK FOR

The CERTIFIED FINANCIAL PLANNER™ (or CFP®) is a designation you receive from the CERTIFIED FINANCIAL PLANNER™ Board of Standards, a nonprofit organization that acts in the public's interest by establishing professional and ethical standards for financial planners. The CFP® Board establishes the education and experience standards that planners must meet and administers the exam a planner must pass to become certified. The board conducts a background check on prospective planners and investigates any complaints from consumers about certified planners. There are about 82,000 CERTIFIED FINANCIAL PLANNER™ practitioners in the United States, but there are only about 3,000 financial planners who have chosen to be part of the National Association of Personal Financial Advisors (NAPFA) and have agreed to abide by their strict fiduciary standard and continuing education requirements.

To find a Fee-Only CERTIFIED FINANCIAL PLANNER™ professional in your area, go to NAPFA.org and click on the Find an Advisor tab. You can search in your geographic area, or you can filter your search to find planners who help a specific type of client—such as unmarried couples, business owners, or medical professionals. You can also filter by technical area, whether its retirement planning, investment advice with ongoing management, or insurance-related issues. You can also filter by fee structure, which includes hourly pay, fixed-fee payments, or an assets-under-management arrangement.

After using that tool to compile a list of potential planners, you can begin researching each of those candidates. The first stop would be SEC.gov. There, you can see if the SEC has ever taken action against one of your candidates, and you can also review each candidate's investment advisor public disclosure (IAPD). These IAPD reports are required when an investment advisor registers and gets licensed through the state or SEC. The SEC advises all investors to review their prospective planner's background. You can quickly see how many jurisdictions someone is registered in and whether that advisor has ever been suspended by any jurisdiction.

On the SEC site, you can also review a detailed report about your candidates. These reports include the investment advisor's employment history, professional qualifications, disciplinary actions, criminal convictions, civil judgments, and arbitration awards. You can also see what their other business activities are, and even if they have rental income or if they volunteer for nonprofit organizations. These documents with the SEC also explain what we do, how we do it, what we get paid, and how we get paid. It also talks about our process.

If you want even more information, you can contact your state securities regulators. You can go to the North American Securities Administrators Association (www.nasaa. org) to find out whom to contact at the state level.

INTERVIEWING POTENTIAL PLANNERS

These reports provide you with some valuable information about a person's interests and experience, but you can learn much more by meeting with your candidates. During that meeting, here are some questions you might ask:

- What kind of experience do you have in retirement planning, tax planning, insurance, and estate planning?
- How do you get paid—hourly, set fee, or a percentage of the amount you have under management? What is your hourly fee and what is your ongoing asset management fee?
- If you charge an asset management fee for overseeing my portfolio, do you charge an hourly fee before that to set up the portfolio?
- Do you earn commissions by selling products?
- Do you have any specialized skills? If so, in what areas have you done advanced training?
- Where have you worked previously?
- How many clients do you typically have?
- Is there a minimum amount that I need to have in my portfolio before you will work with me?
- If I were to hire you to manage my portfolio, how often should I expect to hear from you?

While you may be tempted to ask the financial planner for references, don't be surprised if they decline. I won't give prospective clients the names of my other clients, and I've lost business as a result. I don't view it as my clients' responsibility to take questions about me from total strangers. I take a more private approach and the SEC has stringent rules on how to provide references. In the end, our backgrounds and activities are readily searchable on the internet.

WHAT YOU CAN EXPECT

Once you've selected a financial planner, you can expect to meet or talk with that person a lot in the beginning. To get an overview of your finances, the planner will ask for your banking account statements, tax returns, mutual fund statements, 401(k) statements, estate planning documents—the documents we discussed in chapter 1. Then the planner will want to know more about your goals. Are you conservative or aggressive when it comes to buying stocks? Do you have any charitable intent? Are you in line to receive an inheritance? What kind of insurance do you currently carry and what are the amounts? When do you want to retire? How much do you want to be able to spend in retirement?

From there, I will talk to my new clients about my investment philosophy, and how their portfolio should be structured to meet their goals and timeline. We talk about how government entitlements and taxes should be handled. For some clients, we'll establish a strategy for setting up their retirement paycheck—which accounts will provide the cash, how much cash, and where that cash will be sent for distribution. All told, doing the planning, setting up the accounts, and transferring funds into those accounts can take a while. But don't worry, you'll have someone right there with you to walk you through all the steps.

You don't have to have a million dollars in your 401(k)

to start working with a financial planner. You can begin the planning process early in your career and hire a planner on an hourly basis to help guide you in setting up a savings strategy and an initial retirement plan. Then you can build the relationship over time. Financial planners usually won't start an asset management arrangement with a client until the client has at least $250,000 in their accounts. The amount of time that a good financial planner has to invest early in the relationship to organize and understand a client's financial situation and do the financial planning groundwork necessary to understand each client's unique needs and goals forces planners to set a minimum. Some planners may take on a client with less than $250,000 in their portfolio, but most require a $500,000 or $1 million minimum.

How often I meet with a client varies. I send clients a quarterly report, and some clients come to the office and sit down with me each quarter to go through their portfolio. Other clients, I meet with only once a year, and some have said, "Bob, this is your area of expertise. I'll call or email you if I have any questions."

There are often more meetings in the beginning, and then they taper off as time goes on. With many people, the sessions will resume when they reach life-changing periods—when they start having children, for instance, and want to start a college savings plan, or when they start thinking about retirement or downsizing. I meet with some clients every year to review the retirement plan to ensure that we are still on track and to determine if we need to change anything.

My phone rings more often whenever the stock market drops dramatically, of course. But most of those calls are from new prospects seeking help in the current environment. Most of my clients are comforted in knowing that we have built a portfolio that anticipates the changes in the markets. We talk about it all the time and I continually reference it in the quarterly reports and other communications I send to them.

Some clients call after seeing a report on CNBC that the sky is falling and the bottom is falling out and so on, and the clients are wondering what we should do. Should we sell stocks and move into bonds? Buy gold? In situations like this, people are uncertain and inclined to do the wrong thing. As we've said before, people are hardwired to make the wrong decision.

I explain that the market always has fluctuations. Bear markets are common, and we are prepared for them when they occur. We've armored your portfolio with diversified investments, and we often don't have to make any changes other than rebalancing like I described in chapter 5. We just have to wait out the storm.

One of the critical roles of a financial planner is to bring a broader, historical view of what is happening. Most individual investors don't have the experience to do that, so there is a risk they'll make an emotional decision that hurts them in the long run. I try to provide context and perspective so that I can be the voice of experience and reason when making financial decisions.

PAYING FOR A PLANNER

As we mentioned earlier, there are a couple of ways financial planners can be paid. Some charge an hourly rate, like an attorney, and some charge a flat fee. Those kinds of payments are typical when you are asking a planner to work on a one-time, discrete project for you.

When you have a financial planner manage your portfolio on an ongoing basis, you should expect to pay about 1 percent annually for all the assets managed by that planner. As your assets grow, so does the planner's compensation, so there is a clear incentive for the planner to manage your portfolio wisely. Some financial planners set their percentage based on the size of the portfolio, but the rate should hover around 1 percent in most situations. The money is typically paid out quarterly directly from the account so you don't have to write your financial planner a check.

You also have the option of paying a financial planner on an hourly basis to go through some retirement planning with you and recommend some investments. Then you go off on your own and open up the accounts, fund them, pick the investments, and track them across time. You manage the portfolio and the retirement withdrawals. When I am the asset manager, we still go through all the planning on the front end, but then I guide you and help you open the accounts. I monitor and manage those assets on a regular basis, providing the quarterly reports and making myself available for phone calls or meetings if you have any questions.

Some advisors charge two fees—an up-front financial planning fee to get everything set up and then the ongoing asset management fee. There's nothing wrong with that approach, but I don't work that way; I want to make sure my asset management clients go through the planning process so I can build the right portfolio for them. So for me and the clients I serve in my practice, we do the sometimes time-consuming but revealing financial planning work before we build diversified portfolios that reflect the goals and objectives we identified in the financial planning process. It makes no sense to have a portfolio if it is not built around the goals and objectives you have for your money.

Keep in mind that when you are interviewing financial

planners, they are also interviewing you. The planner wants to make sure your investing philosophies align with their own. I received a call out of the blue one day from a man who said he was interviewing financial planners. He said he had more than a million dollars in assets and had used a planner before, but had severed the arrangement. He said he'd sold his business and would sell his second business as soon as the litigation was over. Then he said he wanted to buy an $800,000 house in Chicago and needed $70,000 in medical treatments. He wrapped it all up by saying he wanted a financial advisor he could argue and debate with.

"So what do you think?" he asked.

"I don't think I would be a good fit for you," I said.

Somewhat taken aback by my bluntness, he asked, "Why not?"

"I'm not looking for clients to argue and debate with."

The point here is that it's a two-way street. I want to work with people who value what I do and whom I feel I can help. I think of it as an informal partnership, not an adversarial relationship. I love working with my clients each and every day and don't want to jeopardize that feeling by taking new clients who don't agree with my fundamental philosophies about financial planning and investing in the stock market.

I'm also leery of prospective clients who are too focused on the fees. I've met with people who have said, "So I have $1 million, and I'll be paying you $10,000 a year. That's a lot of money!" I think these folks are missing the point. Yes, you are paying 1 percent of your assets, but you are getting someone who can counsel you through turbulent times. I don't want to focus too much on returns, but the studies we mentioned earlier also show that good financial planners more than pay for themselves by increasing your portfolio's performance over time. When I look back at the financial crisis of 2007 to 2009, the financial guidance I gave in those times paid for my fees for many years into the future.

You can count on a sound financial planner to keep a steady hand on the tiller when seas get rough, but they offer quite a bit more than that. Their work goes beyond picking stocks. Their guidance, coaching, and support can help you make the best of your life, career, marriage, children, assets, and liabilities. They help you avoid mistakes, manage risk, save time, and get better investment results. They guide you through the maze of retirement options, from 401(k)s and IRAs to pensions and annuities. They'll help you determine the type and amount of insurance you may need to protect you and your family. They'll help you minimize taxes and reduce future tax impacts. If you own a business, they help develop a strategy for managing business finances, whether it's cash flow, financing, employee benefits, or corporate taxes.

Most importantly, they provide the emotional discipline it takes to ensure plans are made, executed, and achieved. They provide guidance, support, reassurance, and stability in a world that seems in short supply of those qualities.

Conclusion

Putting It All Together

I hope I've made retirement planning seem less daunting to you. Although retirement is a significant new stage in your life, the steps I've outlined in this book will make the transition much easier for you. If you're still many years away from retirement, I hope the advice I've offered will guide you on your way to a rich, comfortable life after you leave the workforce.

Among the many ideas to draw from this book are the following:

You are steering the boat. Your retirement will likely be much different than your parents' or grandparents', and to succeed, you must take an active role in planning for retirement. *You* are now responsible for your retirement paycheck—not your employer and not the federal government. These institutions might contribute to your retirement, but determining how much you need and where that money will come from is up to you.

Assess your situation. If you're just starting out in your professional life, start saving now. If you're still ten or fifteen years away, look at your assets and your needs, and increase your savings rate to prepare for the day you retire. If you've already taken the plunge into retirement, invest wisely and avoid emotional decisions.

Get organized. Any valuable retirement plan starts with a clear-eyed assessment of your current financial situation. To make that assessment, prepare a solid net-worth statement, with honest entries about how much you've saved, how much you owe, and how much you need to live on. This will form the foundation of your retirement plan.

Prepare a detailed cash flow statement. Be meticulous about assessing how much you make and how much you spend. If you are still several years away from retirement, this will help you see where you need to make some adjustments by spending less or saving more. If you are close to retirement, this statement will indicate how big your retirement paycheck will need to be.

Plan your trip. Remember, retirement is like taking a vacation. You must decide where you want to go, when you want to leave, and how you are going to pay for it. Identify what you *need* in retirement as well as what you *want* in retirement and then put numbers on those discretionary and nondiscretionary items. Your retirement goals should be realistic, inspiring, and measurable.

Anticipate your future needs. Will you need to pay for weddings in the future? Do you have grandchildren you want to help put through college? Do you have aging parents you might need to care for? Do you have any significant expenses on the horizon? Do you have a rainy day fund set up for emergencies? You must consider and anticipate all of these future needs and wants as you develop your plan.

Plan for catastrophes. Not everyone will lose a spouse or be afflicted with a debilitating disease, but you must plan for these misfortunes anyway. While your life insurance needs decline as you age and your wealth grows, other types of protection may be beneficial to have. If you were to die, how much will your survivors need to cover their expenses? What about long-term care? Insulate yourself against the catastrophes that can wipe out your retirement savings.

Learn the basics of investing. If your retirement paycheck depends in part on the money you make in the stock market, it's vital that you understand the basics. What does it mean to have a diversified portfolio? How much risk can you live with? Why do prominent economists insist that investing should be like watching paint dry? Find out! A basic understanding of investing will help you avoid emotional decisions and allow you to rebalance your investments periodically.

Know your benefits. Social Security is a wonderful benefit for many retirees, but it pays to understand what your rights and obligations are. How much will you owe in taxes during retirement? When should you sign up for Medicare and how much will it cost? Should you have a Roth IRA as well as a traditional one?

Build your paycheck. Most retirees pull money from various sources for their retirement paycheck. There might be a pension, Social Security, investment earnings. Plan that out. What's the best way to take withdrawals from your portfolio? When do required minimum withdrawals start? Find out and plan ahead.

Plan for your passing. Estate planning is the thing no one in the family wants to discuss, but if you want to ensure that your loved ones get all the benefits of your life's work, prepare a will, update the beneficiaries on your various accounts, and anticipate special situations.

A carefully prepared estate plan doesn't require a lot of work, but the benefits of correctly doing it are tremendous. You may need to hire an attorney to accomplish this.

Pick the right advisor. Many financial planners are eager to help you invest your money. But many of them are only interested in selling you products. Fee-Only CERTIFIED FINANCIAL PLANNER™ professionals have your fiduciary interests in mind. They consider all aspects of your life when helping you set up your portfolio and managing your investments. Studies show they don't just pay for themselves but actually deliver higher returns than investors who go it alone.

Retiring isn't easy, and it can seem like a daunting time for many people. That's why I recommend people not only plan for their future retirement but also plan how they want to spend that retirement. Some people play golf every day, and that's great for a while. But then they get bored with golf and they wonder, "What's next?"

Some retirees wake up every morning and the first thing they do is fire up their computer and look at how their portfolio is doing. They do this because part of their retirement paycheck depends on how the stock market is performing. It makes sense to stay on top of your portfolio, of course, but I discourage people from obsessing over it. If the stock market is going through a downturn, constantly examining your portfolio will create a lot of stress in your life and possibly prompt you to make an emotional decision that will hurt you in the long run.

This is why some people choose to continue working part time in retirement, even when they don't have to. A job gives people something to look forward to, and even if your work hours are not as long and stressful as they once were, a part-time job will provide you with a sense of purpose and take your mind off how your portfolio is doing. When you have a job you enjoy, you can lose yourself in your work, stay engaged with the changing world, share your expertise and wisdom with younger coworkers, and enjoy a satisfying sense of accomplishment. And that part-time paycheck makes the stock market seem less important to you.

As I've said before, recessions are as common as dirt. But if you've built a correctly diversified portfolio, you can ride out the downturns. You don't have to make decisions based on the market's gyrations; you make decisions based on your goals and objectives.

A trusted advisor who has your best interests in mind can also ease the transition and make your retirement years much less stressful. To find out more about how an advisor can help you, go to the website for the National Association of Personal Financial Advisors (NAPFA.org) and read about how we can help you. You can use that website to find an advisor in your area, and you can use this book to help you interview some potential candidates!

If you're in the vicinity of one of my offices in Chicago, Cincinnati, or Naples, Florida, please give us a call, and we'll meet. You can look us up at www.g-fg.com and find our phone numbers there, or you can send us a message through the website. You also can read more about the work we do and how we can help you.

But most importantly, enjoy your retirement. You have earned this opportunity to savor life from this new perspective, and I hope this book eases your transition and helps you find the security and contentment you deserve.

Godspeed and fair winds to you and your family on this most important journey.

About the Author

ROBERT GERSTEMEIER is the president and founder of Gerstemeier Financial Group, a Fee-Only investment advisory firm in Chicago, Cincinnati, and Naples, Florida. Bob joined the financial planning profession because he had a sincere desire to provide unbiased counsel and advice to clients to help them realize their financial dreams. Bob is a member of the National Association of Personal Financial Advisors (NAPFA), a Captain in the US Navy Reserves, and volunteers for local charities and community organizations in his hometown of Cincinnati. He and his wife, Laura, have three sons.